Real Estate Investment Trust Investing

The Secret to Passive Income from REITs:
Crush Inflation, Diversify Your Investments
and Avoid Owning Physical Property to Live
Your Dividend Lifestyle

Mike Hartley

Mike Hartley

Real Estate Investment Trust Investing

Disclaimer Notice:

The presented work is strictly informational and should not be interpreted as an offer to buy or sell any form of security, instrument, or investment vehicle. Furthermore, the information contained herein should not be taken as a legal, tax, accounting or investment recommendation given by the author(s) or any affiliated company, employees, or paid contributors. In other words, the information is presented without considering individual preferences for specific investments in terms of risk parameters. It is general information that does not account for a person's lifestyle and financial objectives. It is important to note that no tailored advice will be provided based on the given information.

The authors and their parent company, along with all employees and paid contributors, have agreed to abstain from trading any stock or investment written about for at least two days publication of any new article, book, report, or email. This includes any equity, options, debt, or other instruments related to that security, stock, or company, except for existing orders that pre-existed the submission; all such charges will be disclosed inside the document. The author(s) may have direct or indirect positions in some of the companies mentioned because of holdings in mutual funds, exchange-traded funds, closed-end funds, or other similar vehicles. Such indirect holdings are usually not disclosed as there is no guarantee that the author(s) is aware at any given time of the individual portfolios of any of these funds. Furthermore, certain decisions by these funds, such as buying or selling stocks, could potentially impact an author's position even if it was not done directly by them.

Warning:

There is no simple, easy way to become wealthy, especially regarding investments in the financial markets. While it may be possible to make a significant return on your investment, there is also a high risk of losing a large amount of money if you do not have the proper knowledge and knowledge base. You must conduct thorough research and analysis to succeed with investments with the most significant potential for price appreciation. Investing wisely requires an extensive level of education and an understanding of how markets work for one's portfolio to yield positive returns over time. Before venturing into any investment endeavor, it is essential to consult an experienced financial advisor or professional who can advise what steps should be taken and how much capital should be invested. It is also necessary to review all relevant information about potential investments, such as the company's financial statements and prospectus, to make an informed decision regarding whether to invest. Everyone must remember that past results are not necessarily indicative of future performance, so it is wise never to invest more money than you can afford to lose.

This work is based upon a thorough analysis of SEC filings, current news events, interviews, corporate press releases, and knowledge obtained through our experience as financial traders, investors, journalists, and educators. We encourage readers to be careful when making decisions involving their finances, as they are ultimately responsible for the outcomes of their choices. To ensure they have thoroughly informed themselves before making any investment decisions, we strongly advise readers to take the time to research each subject in more detail by seeking out additional sources such as third-party analysts or other reading materials on the web. Furthermore, we recommend conducting a comprehensive review of all available data to ensure each conclusion is well-rounded and sound by exploring multiple aspects of an issue or topic. Ultimately, we believe that a person's financial future will benefit from making prudent and informed decisions based on knowledge gathered from various sources.

Foreword to the Series

Investing is a necessary and invaluable life skill that many people don't even realize they need. It allows you to create financial stability, accomplish your most ambitious goals, and secure your future. Whether it be providing for loved ones, avoiding the need to work past retirement age, or funding a dream vacation in Japan, investing requires a deep understanding of the principles of finance as well as those of self-discipline, patience, and sound judgement, free from any emotion or prejudice. While this may feel intimidating at first glance, investing can be extremely manageable with the right guidance and strategies that minimize risks while maximizing returns. By staying informed and educated on the basics of investing, we'll have you on the road to financial success.

Whilst this series masquerades as a comprehensive set of educational guides to the various inroads of investing, it is in fact a chronology of what I have learnt over the years - and from almost every aspect of investing there is. Growing up in a family that had relatively few financial resources, I was always driven to make something of myself and ensure the future security of my loved ones. One of the ways I set out to do this was by ambitiously aiming to make a million dollars in cold hard cash - which seems almost comical when I look back on it now as I had no idea why I chose this figure! A million dollars was just an arbitrary number that I decided upon when I didn't fully comprehend what it meant, or how life-changing it could be. I just thought to myself "I think having a sum of money would really help my family along", so, with this goal in mind, I began researching and investing in various different fields; from stocks to bonds to real estate to swing trading, and so on! My journey has been far from easy, but every step along the way has been incredibly rewarding as I've continued to learn about investing and building my wealth. Now, whilst making money is still a priority/hobby for me, having time with my family is what really matters - and is ultimately more satisfying than reaching any arbitrary figure.

Once I had achieved my goal of amassing a million dollars, it was not that such an amount was not enough; on the contrary, it is certainly a significant sum, and having so much money at once gave me a feeling of great accomplishment. However, I found that I didn't want to stop there. It wasn't just about wanting to make more money; it was about wanting to keep on experiencing the joy and sense of fulfilment from investing. As a youth, I had the dream of being rich and financially free, but with more experience, I now invest because I've learnt to love it! After sixteen years of engaging in this activity, I had finally come up with a system which enabled me to make consistent wins with most forms of investing. So, I figured, why should I let this newfound understanding go to waste? Why should I stop now when things were going so well?

When I decided to start learning about investing, I made sure that I was as prepared and organized as possible. I researched thoroughly, making notes on who offered the best services, the cheapest rates, and which brokerages had a reputation for being trustworthy. As someone who is naturally meticulous, it only made sense to take an in-depth approach to this as well. So, I made sticky notes, wrote in journals, and took copious notes in Word documents - all with the intention of compiling my thoughts throughout the process. Fast forward sixteen years later and here I am writing a series of books based on my experiences!

To ensure accuracy when writing this series from different perspectives - such as in 'Investing for Women' - I asked friends and fellow investors for their input to add further insight into each book. In fact, much of what is written regarding investing has been pre-written by me over time in various forms - be it a scribbled note or a more detailed outline of what I personally needed to know to invest in that field. Although not an expert in all areas of investment, through years of research and experience (and help from others!) I have been able to piece together content that reflects a diverse range of perspectives within this field.

Overall, this series of books is an amalgamation of much of my own research and experiences - some of which I have been continuing the entire time — others of which I've found either not profitable, or only mildly profitable, and so I've ditched them in favour of the better-earning ones! I have also included the thoughts, opinions and input from others involved in the investing world, to ensure accurate representation from a variety of perspectives. It has been a fun journey putting together all the pieces and rewarding at the same time. I am excited to share my knowledge and insight into investing with you all.

This series of handbooks provides a comprehensive guide for even the most beginner investor who is looking to start investing with confidence and ease. Each book dives deep into different aspects of investing, providing readers with the essential knowledge and information they need to make smart decisions when it comes to managing their money. These books are tailored specifically for those who want to gain a better understanding of investing in the financial markets and successfully managing their portfolios over time. Despite my American-based viewpoint, anyone can follow the principles explained within these pages regardless of their country. By reading this series from beginning to end, readers will be equipped with all the key tools necessary for success in investing and achieving long-term financial independence.

In addition to straightforward advice on how to invest, this series also offers guidance on everything from basic stock market terminology to more complex financial instruments. Readers will learn about diversification, risk management strategies, cost/benefit analysis, taxes related to investments, and more – giving them a strong foundation of knowledge that can be applied no matter what type of investment they choose.

My goal is for readers not only to understand what's going on in the markets but also to gain insight into why certain strategies have been useful for me, and how you can find the ones that suit you best.

Note:

I'm often asked what investments I'm presently making and it's an important question for those who are seeking to find financial freedom. After giving the matter a great deal of thought, I felt writing this information down in a book would quickly become outdated since I tend to rebalance my investments at least every three months. To provide readers with more up-to-date information, I decided to create a website which will help them understand what I am doing and encourage them to do the same. This website will not only provides details of the investments but also includes facts and figures that illustrate how these strategies can help people achieve their financial objectives. It will offer guidance on how to make wise investment choices and gives insight into the kinds of risk associated with each decision. Furthermore, this website contains detailed advice on how to maximize returns by diversifying your portfolio across multiple asset classes, mitigating losses through careful analysis of market trends, as well as other long-term strategies for achieving financial independence. By taking advantage of all the knowledge provided on this site, readers can feel confident that they have taken steps towards attaining their own financial freedom.

The journey to uncovering the secrets of successful investing can seem daunting, but I'm determined to make it easier for you! By subscribing to my email list, you'll stay up-to-date with the latest books in the series, and eventually be the first to know about my unique investment system. By being on the e-mail list I will also let you know when the website is launched too – exciting! I am constantly thinking "I wish I'd had this when I started! I'd have saved a decade worth of time!"

So, no matter your level of financial literacy, I have comprehensive information for anyone who is keen on learning more. With an array of resources at my disposal, I can give you an in-depth look at the foundation of successful investing. Through these materials, I will provide a thorough look into elements such as risk management principles and best practices, financial forecasting, budgeting techniques, and so much more.

On top of this knowledge base, subscribers will also be given access to exclusive tools such as calculators and other interactive features that can help simplify complex topics like portfolio construction. This way, no matter what your individual goals are when it comes to building wealth through investments - I'm here to help!

By joining my email list you'll have access to all these resources and more. So come on board for this exciting adventure and discover how you can get started investing for success today!

So, with no further ado, let's dive in!

Your Free Bonus Gifts

Accelerate Your **Learning**

Maximize Your **Earning**

We are here to help you crush it – no bones about it. To make the most of this book, there are two things you'll need:

1. **FREE RESOURCES**

   We have created a number of free resources for you to take advantage of. Use them to accelerate your learning and maximize your earning!

2. **FURTHER RESOURCES**

   We are constantly striving to continue supporting both our team and our students. We are busy creating a website to better highlight all of our investing tips, tricks and current holdings to help our users better see what we're actually up to! To find out when we launch this, and be alerted when we release other titles, just subscribe to our e-mail list and you'll be the first to know!

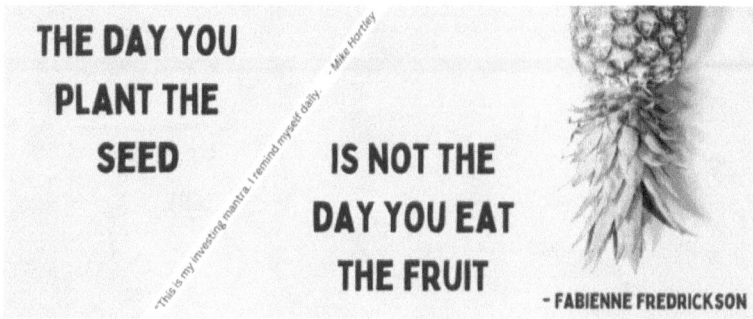

Subscribe To The Newsletter and Join Us!

- Find out the secrets to investing safely
- Join the growing **FIRE** (**F**inancially **I**ndependent **R**etire **E**arly) Movement!
- Live your passive income lifestyle…

www.thefirefund.com/free-gift

Table of Contents

Mike Hartley

Introduction

The best investment on earth is earth.

–Louis J. Glickman

As you wander around a bustling city setting, observing the remarkable skyscrapers and chic shopping centers that compose its environment, has the thought of owning a fraction of these exceptional edifices ever crossed your mind?

Real Estate Investment Trusts (REITs) offer a means to attain such a goal. By investing in REITs, a variety of property types become accessible, including office buildings, residential complexes, and storage units. This book aims to guide you through the enthralling domain of REIT investing while assisting you in deciphering the complexities of this distinct and potentially profitable investment approach.

> If you choose to venture into the world of REITs, you may encounter obstacles such as grasping its fundamentals, navigating the array of property types, and pinpointing the ideal REITs for your investment goals.

It's also possible that you might face challenges when

interpreting financial benchmarks and ratios crucial for evaluating REITs or feel concerned about liquidity and related risks. Furthermore, adapting to ever-changing real estate market conditions and the impact of economic factors on your investments could be a source of unease. Rest assured; this book aims to provide clarity on these concerns.

By reading this book, you can expect to gain a variety of valuable benefits and results, such as:

- Grasping the basics of REITs: Acquire a solid foundation of REIT knowledge, including their structures, varieties, and operations, empowering you to make well-informed investment choices.

- Broadening your investments: Uncover ways to diversify your portfolio with REITs, minimizing risks while maximizing your potential for strong returns.

- Generating passive income: Enjoy the regular dividends distributed by REITs, which provide you with a consistent source of passive earnings.

- Learning from the experts: Take advantage of the wisdom shared by seasoned investors and industry insiders, ensuring you adopt effective approaches when investing in REITs.

- Protecting against inflation: Recognize how REIT investments can serve as a buffer against inflation, maintaining their worth as real estate typically appreciates over time.

- Benefiting from tax perks: Explore the tax advantages linked to REIT investing, potentially enhancing your overall returns.

- Identifying growth opportunities: Understand how to pinpoint high-growth potential REITs that can boost your investment portfolio's long-term performance.

Should you choose to embrace the advice presented in this book, you'll be ready to adeptly explore the world of REIT investing, taking advantage of real estate investment opportunities to create a more stable and flourishing financial path for yourself.

Having gained valuable knowledge and hands-on experience in real estate and finance, I ventured through the investment world, engaging with a diverse range of property types throughout their journey. I also dedicated substantial time to staying informed about the latest trends and progress in REITs. My background, coupled with (I've been told) my ability to make complex ideas easily understandable and enjoyable, positions me as a capable guide for those seeking to learn about REIT investing.

As we wrap up the introduction, we're prepared to dive further into the enthralling domain of real estate investing. In the upcoming chapter, we'll unravel core ideas, enhance our comprehension of the sector, and lay a solid foundation for our REIT investment odyssey. So, let's flip the page and set off on this enlightening voyage together.

CHAPTER 1

Discovering the World of Real Estate Investment

Buy real estate in areas where the path exists and buy more real estate where there is no path, but you can create your own.

–David Waronker

Imagine a sector where investing in real estate is as simple as purchasing stocks or bonds without the burden of managing physical properties or pouring enormous capital into a single asset. This is the fascinating world of Real Estate Investment Trusts.

Throughout this chapter, we will shed light on the enigmatic world of REITs. We'll journey through their origins and development, analyzing their historical performance and highlighting significant milestones and groundbreaking evolutions. We'll investigate the ways REITs create income for investors, expound on the benefits of investing in them, and demonstrate how they can contribute to a well-balanced investment portfolio. Finally, we'll tackle the topic of liquidity, determining whether REITs should be classified as liquid or illiquid investments. So, get comfortable and prepare to embark on an enlightening expedition into the domain of REITs, where the door to real estate investment is opened wide for everyone.

What Are REITs?

REITs offer you the chance to reap the rewards of property investments without the usual responsibilities that come with being a property owner. Fundamentally, REITs are organizations that possess and handle income-producing real estate properties, encompassing a diverse array of assets such as residential buildings, retail establishments, hospitality facilities, and work environments (Chen, 2023). The charm of REITs is rooted in their capability to provide a consistent revenue stream for investors. This characteristic makes REITs particularly attractive for individuals seeking a dependable source of passive income.

Two primary categories of REITs exist: equity REITs and mortgage REITs. Equity REITs own and operate physical properties, whereas mortgage REITs concentrate their investments on mortgages and mortgage-linked securities. In general, equity REITs are more sought after due to their closer association with real estate properties.

Engaging in REIT investments is as straightforward as purchasing shares of a publicly-traded REIT through a brokerage account, much like acquiring stocks. This ease of entry renders REITs an appealing choice for various investors, even those with limited real estate investing experience.

Nonetheless, it's important to acknowledge that, as with any investment, REITs involve specific uncertainties. Factors such as economic changes, fluctuations in property values, and interest rate shifts can all affect a REIT's performance. For this reason, it is crucial to undertake thorough research and assess your investment goals before delving into REIT investments.

Origin and Evolution of REITs

REITs first emerged in the United States in 1960, following the enactment of the Real Estate Investment Trust Act by Congress. The aim was to make property investment accessible to the average investor. This groundbreaking law created a unique type of corporation that could own and manage real estate assets that generated income while allowing individual investors to profit through share acquisition (*History of REITs*, n.d.).

Over time, the allure of REITs increased as investors realized their ability to consistently generate income and add diversification to their portfolios. With the global expansion of this industry came a broader range of assets managed by REITs, going beyond residential, retail, and office properties to encompass specialized assets like data centers, cell towers, and healthcare facilities.

As REITs matured, various types emerged, with the aforementioned equity REITs and mortgage REITs becoming the two main categories. Over time, investors have tended to favor equity REITs because of their direct connection to real estate assets.

In the present day, we have observed the development of both publicly-traded and non-traded REITs, presenting investors with diverse levels of liquidity and risk exposure. Publicly-traded REITs, listed on stock exchanges, provide higher liquidity and transparency, while non-traded REITs, although less liquid, might yield higher dividends in certain situations.

In recent times, technology's impact on the real estate industry has also affected the progression of REITs. Cutting-edge property technology, known as PropTech, is changing how properties are managed, bought, and sold. Consequently, REITs have had to adapt to these technological advances to remain competitive and continue delivering value to investors.

A History of REIT Performance

As touched upon earlier, Real Estate Investment Trusts first appeared on the scene in the United States in 1960. This cutting-edge investment approach allowed individuals to engage in profit-oriented real estate ventures, creating a myriad of fresh possibilities. Over the years, REITs have displayed exceptional endurance and flexibility, successfully navigating market upheavals and economic hardships.

During the 1970s and 1980s, the REIT market faced its first hurdles as interest rates soared and the real estate industry witnessed a downturn. Despite this, REITs soldiered on, concentrating on the income-generating aspect of their investments. Their resolve became evident in the ensuing boom of the 1990s, when REITs experienced a resurgence, benefiting from economic prosperity and advantageous market conditions.

Entering the 21st century, REITs encountered yet another challenge in the form of the 2008 Great Recession. The worldwide financial crisis had a profound effect on the real estate sector, impacting REIT performance. However, history reveals that these investment trusts demonstrated adaptability once again. As the economy rebounded, REITs recovered their footing, driven by renewed enthusiasm for real estate projects and market growth (*REITs prove resilient*, n.d.).

Throughout their existence, REITs have exhibited an impressive ability to produce income for investors. The regular distribution of dividends, a hallmark of REITs, has been instrumental in their overall success. For those seeking a relatively stable investment with a continuous income stream, REITs have proven to be an attractive choice.

Lately, a rising worldwide fascination with environmentally conscious and ethically sound investments has been observed. This trend has not gone unnoticed by the REIT industry. Many REITs have now shifted their focus to environmental, social, and governance (ESG) considerations, making them an appealing option for conscientious investors.

Looking back on the history of REIT performance, it becomes evident that these investment vehicles have withstood challenges and emerged stronger with each passing trial. Amidst constantly evolving markets, their adaptability, fortitude, and dedication to generating income have made them a reliable selection for investors.

Major Milestones and Key Developments in the REIT Industry

The REIT sector has displayed exceptional endurance and flexibility, successfully navigating a myriad of market trials and economic shifts.

A key moment in REIT history transpired during the early 1990s when the industry witnessed a revitalization. This was partly attributable to the establishment of the UPREIT (Umbrella Partnership Real Estate Investment Trust) framework in 1992. This inventive model allowed property proprietors to exchange their real estate assets for operating partnership units (OP units), effectively postponing capital gains taxes. The UPREIT structure encouraged the expansion of the REIT sector by drawing new investors and fostering growth (deBree, n.d.).

A significant additional development in the REIT field occurred in 2001, when the Global Industry Classification Standard (GICS) acknowledged real estate as an independent asset class. This recognition further validated REITs as an investment instrument and enticed a more varied investor demographic.

Upon reflecting on the critical milestones and prominent developments in the REIT sector, it's evident that this distinctive investment mechanism has transformed considerably since its origin. Through versatility, persistence, and devotion to income production, REITs have time and again proven their worth to investors. As the industry carries on with its growth and adaptation, it will undoubtedly continue to be a vital and dependable option for investors pursuing income and diversification in their portfolios.

How REITs Generate Income for Investors

As you know by now, REITs are organizations that possess, operate, or finance properties that generate revenue. By pooling the resources of numerous investors, these companies enable access to a more extensive array of real estate investments than individual investors might achieve independently. In this way, even those with modest means can participate in the often-rewarding real estate sector.

A primary way REITs create income for investors is through the rental revenue from the properties under their ownership. For example, if a REIT owns an apartment complex, the tenants' rent payments contribute to the REIT's overall income. This revenue is subsequently distributed to investors as regular dividends. The advantage of this setup is that investors obtain a portion of the rental income without bearing the responsibility of managing the properties.

Another income stream for REITs arises from the potential increase in the value of the real estate assets they hold. Although property values can fluctuate, carefully selected assets tend to appreciate over time. When a REIT sells a property at a higher price than its purchase cost, the resulting profit is divided among the investors. However, it's important to remember that most REITs primarily focus on income generation through rental revenue, so capital appreciation should be viewed as a supplementary benefit rather than the central objective.

Some REITs also invest in mortgage-backed securities or offer financing to property developers rather than directly owning properties. This category of REIT may appeal to investors seeking exposure to real estate without the associated risks of property ownership and management.

REITs must legally distribute a minimum of 90% of their taxable income to shareholders as dividends. Consequently, investors can typically anticipate consistent income from their REIT investments. Nonetheless, as with all investments, risks are involved. Conducting thorough research on individual REITs and the broader real estate market is crucial for making prudent decisions.

Portfolio Diversification With REITs

Throughout this book, you might have observed that "portfolio diversification" is a vital concept when it comes to REITs.

To build a robust investment portfolio, it's crucial to include various assets with different risk and return potentials. This approach helps you spread the risk, so if one type of investment falters, others can balance the effects. Incorporating REITs into your portfolio enables diversification in both asset classes and geographical areas.

REITs prove valuable for diversification as they frequently show a low correlation with other investments such as stocks and bonds. This means that REITs' performance is not directly tied to stock market changes, offering an additional level of risk control.

When you invest in REITs, you collaborate with other investors, granting access to a more extensive array of properties and further diversification within the real estate realm. You can also opt for equity REITs, which own and manage properties, or mortgage REITs, which finance real estate. This adaptability lets you customize your portfolio to strike the right balance between income generation and capital appreciation.

Another advantage of investing in REITs is their professional management. Skilled managers with profound real estate market knowledge oversee REITs' operations, which is a significant benefit for individual investors who may not have the time or expertise to manage properties on their own. This expert direction can boost your confidence in your investments.

Integrating REITs into your investment portfolio provides numerous advantages, such as diversification across asset classes and within the real estate sector, professional management, and the potential for income generation. By including REITs in your portfolio, you can more effectively manage risks and broaden your investment possibilities. So, when you're looking for ways to expand your investment scope, remember the essential role REITs can fulfill in your diversification plans.

Are REITs Liquid or Illiquid?

> Liquidity plays a crucial role when evaluating investments, as it signifies how effortlessly an investment can be purchased or sold without causing substantial price shifts.

In the case of REITs, you may be curious about their liquidity. Let's delve into this subject to enhance your understanding.

There are predominantly two categories of REITs: publicly-traded and non-traded. The liquidity of each varies, so it's essential to recognize these distinctions.

Publicly-traded REITs are available on stock exchanges, which allows for easy buying and selling, much like stocks. A notable benefit of investing in publicly-traded REITs is their elevated liquidity, as they can be exchanged promptly with minimal influence on their pricing. This feature offers investors the ability to smoothly transition in and out of positions, making these REITs a desirable option for those who appreciate adaptability in their investments.

On the other hand, non-traded REITs are not found on stock exchanges, rendering them more complex to buy and sell. Consequently, they are considered illiquid investments. This reduced liquidity can create hurdles for investors, particularly when they need to access their funds quickly. It's crucial to weigh the possible challenges linked to non-traded REITs' illiquidity against the potential advantages before investing.

The allure of potentially higher returns can make non-traded REITs an attractive option for some investors when compared with their publicly-traded counterparts. However, these increased returns carry greater risks, including illiquidity. Additionally, non-traded REITs often come with elevated fees and decreased transparency compared to their publicly-traded equivalents (Copeland, 2021).

While taking liquidity into account is important when examining REITs, other aspects should be considered as well. These factors encompass the REITs' overall performance, dividend yields, and management quality, along with your distinct financial objectives and risk tolerance.

In conclusion, REITs' liquidity is contingent upon whether they are publicly-traded or not. Publicly-traded REITs provide high liquidity, making them fit for investors who value the ability to rapidly buy and sell their investments. Non-traded REITs, conversely, are illiquid, which can pose difficulties for investors requiring fast access to their funds. Nonetheless, non-traded REITs may offer higher returns, making them alluring to investors ready to embrace additional risks, including illiquidity.

Before opting to invest in REITs, thoroughly assess the liquidity of the specific REIT type as well as other factors like performance, dividend yields, and management competence. By dedicating time to learning the nuances of various REITs, you can make informed decisions that correspond with your financial goals and risk tolerance.

Key Takeaways

- Two main REIT types exist: Equity REITs, which deal with physical properties, and mortgage REITs, which focus on mortgages and related securities.

- Diving into REITs is a breeze, as simple as purchasing stocks via a brokerage account, which appeals to investors of all levels and backgrounds.

- Although REITs offer a consistent income stream, they're not without risks, so research and goal assessment are crucial before investing.

- REITs have evolved over time, with regulations and technology shaping their growth, resulting in various types and a focus on environmental, social, and governance considerations.

Chapter Summary

Over time, Real Estate Investment Trusts incorporated technology, novel asset types, and ESG factors, further enhancing their appeal to investors. Featuring various REIT classifications and a dedication to steady income production, these investment tools present an enticing chance to diversify your portfolio and reap the rewards of the real estate market.

Keep in mind that, as with all investments, it's crucial to research thoroughly and evaluate your objectives to make the most fitting choice for your financial journey.

After getting familiar with the foundations of REITs, we're ready to venture further and uncover the assortment of categories that exist. In the chapter ahead, we'll traverse the colorful landscape of REITs, offering you a clearer view of their individual attributes and helping you pinpoint the ones that resonate with your financial objectives. Onward we go to broaden your knowledge!

CHAPTER 2

Exploring Different Types of REITs

Buy land, they're not making it anymore.

–Mark Twain

Imagine a world where you could invest in various real estate opportunities while sitting in your favorite chair sipping coffee. The fascinating world of REITs offers you this opportunity, so let's dive into the different types that are waiting for you!

Each one comes with distinct characteristics and advantages, making it crucial to grasp them so you can determine which one aligns with your financial objectives.

We'll begin by looking at equity REITs, the most prevalent form of REIT. Understand how they invest in properties, produce income, and share profits with investors, letting you enjoy the benefits of real estate investments without hands-on involvement.

Next, we'll examine mortgage REITs and how they stand apart from equity-focused ones. Learn how mortgage REITs create income by investing in mortgage-backed securities, providing an alternative approach to real estate investing.

Finally, we'll explore hybrid REITs, a special combination of both equity and mortgage REITs. If you're pumped, let's jump right in and start this chapter.

Types of REITs

In this section, we'll investigate the trio of main REIT categories: equity, mortgage, and hybrid. By discussing the unique features, approaches to investing, and ways of generating income that each type offers, you'll acquire essential knowledge to inform your investment choices (Chen, 2023).

Equity REIT

Venturing into the realm of investment, one might come across an intriguing player—the Equity Real Estate Investment Trust. It's a distinctive investment avenue that provides an opportunity to have a stake in the real estate sector without the need to directly own any property.

Equity REITs are corporations that possess, manage, or finance revenue-yielding real estate. Their reach can extend over various types of properties, encompassing everything from shopping centers and office buildings to apartment complexes and storage units. They put their capital into these properties with the goal of creating a source of income.

The process through which these equity REITs create revenue is truly captivating. They don't solely rely on property sales for profit, although that can occasionally contribute. Their main source of revenue stems from leasing their properties and receiving rent from occupants. This ensures a consistent flow of income, which is a striking feature of this type of investment.

What further enhances the allure of equity REITs for investors is their method of profit allocation. They're legally bound, as mentioned earlier, to distribute about 90% of their revenue to their shareholders every year in the form of dividends. This attribute makes them a lucrative option for those seeking a regular influx of income from their investments.

In essence, equity REITs, with their unique investment strategy in real estate, income generation mechanisms, and profit distribution practices, offer a viable entryway into the world of real estate investment.

Mortgage REITs

Unlike their counterparts, equity REITs and mortgage REITs don't focus on owning and leasing physical properties. In contrast, their primary focus is real estate financing, particularly by purchasing mortgages and mortgage-backed securities.

The inner workings of mortgage REITs involve accumulating capital, which is then invested in purchasing existing mortgages or mortgage-backed securities. These securities are essentially a collection of home loans that financial institutions consolidate and sell to investors. Revenue generation for mortgage REITs primarily stems from the interest borrowers pay on these loans, providing a stream of income that does not rely on property rents.

The distinction between mortgage REITs and equity REITs lies in their investment strategies. While equity REITs function like property owners, collecting rent from tenants, mortgage REITs operate similarly to financial institutions, extending loans and earning from interest payments. Both offer distinct ways to invest in the property market without the need for direct property ownership.

Nonetheless, it's essential to note that mortgage REITs carry their own distinct set of risks and benefits. Usually, changes in interest rates have a significant impact on their performance.

Should interest rates rise, the value of current mortgage-backed securities often decreases. Conversely, a decrease in rates typically signals an increase in the value of these securities. Therefore, investment in mortgage REITs calls for a strong understanding of the wider interest rate climate and the factors that might sway it.

Mortgage REITs present an intriguing pathway for those interested in the property sector but who are more inclined towards its financial aspects than dealing with physical properties. By putting money into mortgage-backed securities, these trusts offer a distinct method to derive income from real estate.

Hybrid REITs

Now, there's a certain category of real estate investment trusts that marries the attributes of its two counterparts: equity REITs and mortgage REITs. This compelling class is recognized as hybrid REITs.

Hybrid REITs dive into the dual arenas of owning physical real estate (a trait of equity REITs) and holding mortgage-backed securities (a characteristic of mortgage REITs). Consider them the best of both worlds, allowing investors to explore both the terrain of property ownership and the landscape of real estate finance.

The strategy of hybrid REITs is to mix their investments between properties that generate income and mortgage-backed securities that yield interest. This blend has the potential to yield a stable stream of income while tempering the overall risk profile.

Revenue generation for hybrid REITs emanates from two key sources. On the one hand, they accumulate rental income from the properties they manage, akin to equity REITs. On the other hand, they receive interest from the mortgage-backed securities they possess, mirroring mortgage REITs. This twin-source income model often renders hybrid REITs an attractive proposition for those seeking varied revenue avenues.

Yet, as with any investment, hybrid REITs come with their own set of hurdles. Primarily, these REITs shoulder the risks tied to both property stewardship and mortgage lending, such as potential drops in property value, tenant disputes, and interest rate changes that can sway the worth of their mortgage-backed securities.

Additionally, the intricacy of handling a hybrid portfolio poses another challenge. It calls for expertise in both property oversight and investment in mortgage-backed securities. Not all REITs may possess the necessary skill set to manage such an eclectic portfolio effectively, which may impact the performance of the investment.

Lastly, the very diversification that makes hybrid REITs enticing can also serve as a disadvantage. If an investor seeks concentrated exposure to either physical properties or mortgage-backed securities, a hybrid REIT may not fit the bill. Instead, a more focused investment in either an equity REIT or a mortgage REIT could be more suitable.

To sum it up, hybrid REITs provide an interesting blend of equity and mortgage REITs' features. They offer a unique avenue for diversification and dual income sources, but they also carry their own set of challenges.

Key Takeaways

- Equity REITs are your ticket to the real estate market without the hassle of property ownership. They make their dough by leasing properties and sharing the income with you, the investor.

- Mortgage REITs are the financiers of the group, earning their keep from interest on real estate loans. But beware: Changes in interest rates can dramatically affect their performance.

- Hybrid REITs are multitaskers, dabbling in both property ownership and mortgage lending. They have a diverse income stream but also face a broader range of risks.

- When it comes to hybrid REITs, you're dealing with the ups and downs of both property management and real estate finance. It's a balancing act.

- Knowing your REITs—equity, mortgage, and hybrid—is like having a roadmap to the real estate investment world. Each has its own unique income-generating strategies and associated risks, so it's key to know what you're getting into.

Chapter Summary

This chapter took you on a deep dive into the world of REITs, highlighting their distinct flavors: equity, mortgage, and hybrid. Equity REITs are the property moguls of the investment sphere, owning and leasing properties to rake in the rent. Mortgage REITs, by contrast, are the money lenders earning from the interest on real estate loans. Hybrid REITs? They're the all-rounders, owning properties and providing loans. This gives them multiple income streams, but with that comes a wider spectrum of risks. The real estate investment journey is filled with opportunities and pitfalls, and understanding the characteristics of each type of REIT is your first step towards navigating this complex terrain.

Having explored the various types of REITs, let's dive even deeper. Up next, we're going to break down the structure, regulation, and trading of these real estate investments. We'll also check out private REITs, Real Estate Operating Companies, and other investment alternatives. Ready to level up your knowledge? Onward we go!

CHAPTER 3

Real Estate Investment Options

Investing should be more like watching paint dry or watching grass grow. If you want excitement, take $800 and go to Las Vegas.

–Paul Samuelson

Ever thought about how some people seem to effortlessly navigate the vast realm of real estate investing? It's not magic; it's REITs, and this is your invitation to join the party!

Have you heard about publicly-traded REITs? They're like the popular kids at school—the ones everyone knows. They live by the rules of the stock exchange and are traded just like any other stock you might fancy.

But don't let popularity fool you; the underdogs have their charm too. Enter private REITs, the less visible but equally intriguing alternative, bringing their own set of advantages and challenges to the table. And we can't forget the cousins—the Real Estate Operating Companies. They may not be REITs, but they've got their own unique playbook.

This chapter is your ticket to a journey that will take you deep into the heart of real estate and its competitive investments.

We'll be exploring bonds, convertible bonds, preferred stocks, and other enticing high-yielding equities. You'll get insights into how to achieve impressive total returns, how to fine-tune your portfolio for the best risk-adjusted returns, and how to use liquidity, inflation hedging, and transparent corporate structures to your advantage. This journey is about to get exciting!

Publicly-Traded REITs

Publicly-traded REITs strut their stuff on the big stage, getting traded on major stock exchanges alongside those popular tech or retail stocks you know and love.

First up, let's break down their structure. Publicly-traded REITs generally take the form of corporations or business trusts. They gather funds from a multitude of investors and use this capital to acquire, oversee, and sell real estate assets that generate income. It's like the glammed-up, red-carpet version of real estate investing, open to everyday people just like yourself.

Since they're publicly-traded, these REITs need to abide by Securities and Exchange Commission (SEC) regulations. That means they're required to submit financial reports regularly and undergo audits, similar to any other publicly-traded company. Plus, they must adhere to specific IRS guidelines to keep their REIT status intact.

When it comes to purchasing and selling shares in publicly-traded REITs, it's a breeze. Say you're on your go-to online brokerage platform, eyes scanning for that unique REIT ticker symbol. Found it? Great! Click, and you're ready to buy or sell shares at the live market price. It's that straightforward; no magic tricks or secret handshakes are needed. Their presence on major exchanges makes them highly liquid, allowing for the swift and easy buying or selling of shares (CFI Team, 2023).

But don't get too comfy! Publicly-traded REITs also come with their fair share of risks. The financial scale measuring your investment doesn't stay still; it bobs up and down, influenced by general market vibes, interest rate movements, and how well those foundational real estate assets are doing. Merely tucking your cash into an investment and turning a blind eye won't cut it. You've got to stay in the loop, monitor the broader market trends, and understand its highs and lows. After all, being in the know is half the battle!

Private REITs

Starting your journey into real estate investing might feel like setting sail into uncharted waters, especially with the sea of investment options out there. Among these, a less talked-about but potentially beneficial choice is private Real Estate Investment Trusts.

Before embarking, let's get acquainted with the fundamentals. A private REIT is a unique investment vehicle that allows investors to combine their resources to invest in properties that generate income. Unlike public REITs that you'd find listed on a stock exchange, private REITs are off-market and usually extended to accredited investors through private placements. Now, this might sound a bit exclusive, but if you have the financial credentials outlined by the SEC, private REITs could be your treasure trove.

The standout feature of private REITs is the possibility of higher returns. Being immune to the typical market swings that affect public REITs, these can offer a more consistent and potentially rewarding investment. Plus, they often show a lower correlation to the stock and bond markets, offering an additional layer of diversification for your portfolio.

However, just like any adventurous journey, there are challenges to consider. With private REITs, you could face higher fees, partly due to the lack of the same regulatory checks and balances as public REITs. This could also result in less transparency, adding a layer of difficulty to evaluating the investment and its management.

Another crucial aspect to consider is liquidity. Given their private status, offloading your investment in a private REIT might not be smooth sailing. The exit routes could vary, and you might have to endure a long waiting period or accept a discounted value for your shares.

So, where does this leave private REITs? Ultimately, it comes down to your risk appetite, financial goals, and circumstances. If you're an accredited investor with an eye for diversification and potentially higher returns, private REITs could be a great addition to your investment map. But remember, weighing the advantages and disadvantages, doing your research, and consulting with a seasoned advisor are key to making an informed decision (*Skyline wealth explains*, n.d.).

The Benefits and Drawbacks of Investing in Private REITs

Let's play a bit of financial hopscotch, leaping into more of the pros and cons of private REITs. They offer a unique blend of rewards and challenges, and understanding these can help you invest prudently.

Pros

- **Potential for higher returns**: Not being at the mercy of public markets can lead to generous yields.

- **Diversification of your portfolio**: Unique properties in the mix can make your financial spread more interesting.

- **Reduced market volatility**: Not being publicly-traded insulates these investment vehicles from daily market swings.

Cons

- **Lack of transparency**: Without public trading, information is not as readily accessible, making evaluation harder.

- **Limited liquidity**: Selling your shares might not be quick or at the price you'd like.

- **Higher entry point**: The minimum investment is usually higher, potentially out of reach for some.

- **Aimed at accredited investors**: Specific income or net worth criteria need to be met to participate.

Real Estate Operating Companies

Real Estate Operating Companies, popularly known as REOCs, open up an alternate avenue to those with an eye for real estate investment. Their playground is quite similar to REITs, touching upon diverse assets like offices, shopping hubs, residential apartments, and hotels. Yet, when it comes to the operational blueprint and business strategy, REOCs stand apart from REITs.

REOCs aren't just about investing in real estate for income generation, unlike REITs. These are firms that take the ownership and management of their real estate assets quite seriously, with the clear aim of asset growth. They channel their earnings back into the business, perhaps by acquiring more properties or upgrading the existing ones. They play for the long haul, focusing on inflating the company's worth over time rather than dolling out immediate returns to investors.

> The regulatory landscape for REOCs is distinct from that of REITs. There is no mandate for them to shell out a fixed percentage of their taxable income as dividends to investors.

This may seem like a shortcoming for those seeking a regular income stream, but the silver lining here is the reinvestment potential. With REOCs retaining a larger chunk of their profits, they have ample capital for business reinvestment. This can catalyze considerable growth over time, potentially leading to a rise in share value.

However, every investment avenue comes with its share of potholes, and REOCs are no exception. While they aim for growth, not every investment yields the desired fruit. If a property acquisition or an upgrade project fails to deliver the projected returns, it can dent the company's profits and, subsequently, the stock's value. Moreover, since REOCs often shoulder more debt to finance their growth, they may be more exposed to economic downturns.

Investing in REOCs feels a lot like investing in other kinds of businesses. As an investor, you're placing your bet on the company's potential to grow and escalate its value over time. This contrasts with investing in REITs, where the focus is more on the income that the real estate properties churn out.

Though REOCs and REITs both orbit around real estate, they present unique opportunities and risks. And as with any investment, comprehending these is key to making informed decisions. So, take a good look at your financial goals, risk tolerance, and investment horizon before deciding if REOCs fit the bill for your portfolio.

Real Estate and Competitor Investment

Real estate and REITs offer a sense of solidity. You're investing in physical assets, and these assets can appreciate over time.

Plus, with rental properties or REITs, you're looking at potential regular income from rents.

Bonds, including convertible bonds, offer a steadier, less risky ride. They provide a fixed income over time, which makes them a reliable, though often less profitable, investment. However, real estate might edge them out when it comes to potential returns and the ability to hedge against inflation.

Convertible bonds have the possibility of converting into stocks, thus offering a chance for higher returns. However, they still don't offer the tangible security of real estate or the income potential of rent.

Preferred stocks do have a higher claim on earnings and assets than common stocks, but they don't offer the same potential for appreciation that real estate does. They also can't provide rental income, like REITs or rental properties.

Other high-yielding equities can provide significant returns but often at a higher risk. Real estate, while not without its risks, offers both potential appreciation and rental income, making it a balanced choice between risk and reward.

Double-digit total returns are an ambitious goal that both real estate and high-yielding equities could reach, but they require a higher risk tolerance. Real estate can offer such returns, especially in booming markets or successful REITs.

Portfolio diversification is key to a balanced investment strategy. Real estate, particularly through REITs, can be a part of this strategy, providing a balance between the volatility of equities and the lower returns of bonds.

In terms of superior risk-adjusted returns, real estate can shine. It offers the potential for high returns while also providing a tangible asset and steady income from rents.

Liquidity can be a challenge in real estate. Selling a property can take time, and REITs might be subject to market conditions. Bonds and equities generally offer higher liquidity, but they lack the tangible security of real estate.

When inflation starts nudging the cost of your everyday items upward, you can count on your real estate investments, whether in property value or rental income, to follow a similar trajectory. This is a feature that bonds, with their fixed returns, can't offer.

Transparent corporate structures are essential to any investment. REITs, in particular, are required to follow certain regulations, providing a level of transparency that investors can appreciate.

So, while every investment has its pros and cons, real estate—and REITs in particular—offer a unique blend of benefits that can make them a powerful player in a balanced portfolio.

Key Takeaways

- Publicly-traded REITs, traded on major stock exchanges, bring real estate within reach. Yet their value is swayed by market dynamics, necessitating informed decision-making.

- Private REITs are a less-explored avenue for accredited investors, promising higher returns and portfolio diversification. Be prepared for challenges like reduced transparency, increased fees, and potential liquidity issues.

- Offering a unique take on real estate investment, REOCs prioritize asset value growth over immediate income. They have the potential for expansion but bear their own set of risks, including vulnerability to economic downturns.

  When weighed against bonds, convertible bonds, and preferred stocks, real estate offers the dual advantage of asset appreciation and continuous income, contributing robustly to your diversified portfolio.

Chapter Summary

This chapter navigates the multifaceted landscape of real estate investments. It started by delving into publicly-traded REITs, your ticket to the grand performance of real estate investment. They were presented as easy to trade but susceptible to market fluctuations.

Next, the journey led us to the world of private REITs, a somewhat secretive sphere reserved for accredited investors. They offered an enticing promise of superior returns and a diversified portfolio. However, navigating this path required careful consideration of aspects like high fees and liquidity issues.

This chapter introduced Real Estate Operating Companies, a unique concept in real estate investing. These companies emphasized the long-term growth of asset value, leading to promising possibilities. However, they came with inherent risks, such as a higher vulnerability to economic downturns.

In this part of the book, we also examined how real estate fared when pitted against other forms of investment. The narrative made a compelling case for real estate as a solid contributor to a diversified portfolio, offering both regular income and potential appreciation.

Finally, we highlighted how real estate could be a dependable ally in the face of inflation. When everyday expenses started to rise, real estate investments, whether in property value or rental income, were likely to follow suit, offering a shield against the rising tide of inflation.

CHAPTER 4

The Investment Process in REITs

Opportunities come infrequently. When it rains gold, put out the bucket, not the thimble.

–Warren Buffett

Have you ever wondered how to become a player in the REIT market? This chapter is your game plan. We will demystify the steps to investing in REITs and illuminate the path to diversification in this exciting asset class.

This chapter isn't about scratching the surface; we're going deep into the trenches. We'll explore everything from the art of researching REITs to setting up a brokerage account and then mastering the dance of buying and selling REIT shares.

But the journey doesn't stop at buying. We'll explore the considerations you need to make before investing, such as evaluating a REIT's financial performance, understanding the importance of management quality, and considering the impact of market conditions.

Finally, we'll cap off this chapter with a discussion on diversification, a crucial strategy in any investment plan. This chapter is going to shed light on the crucial aspect of sprucing up your REIT portfolio through diversification. You'll learn ingenious tactics to spread your investments across the REIT landscape and even beyond, encompassing other real estate ventures and diverse asset classes. After all, variety is the spice of investment life!

So, are you ready to start your journey towards becoming a savvy REIT investor? Let's dive in!

How to Invest in REITs

Not everyone has the assets to jump straight into the real estate market, but REITs? They provide a platform for equal opportunity for a broader audience. Here's how to get your slice of the financial pie:

- Step one: Arm yourself with knowledge. Imagine a REIT as a firm that owns, operates, and manages a wide variety of real estate assets. Imagine being able to snag a portion of this firm. That's your ticket into real estate investment without the hassles of owning an actual property.

- Step two: Do your research. You'll come across different categories of REITs: residential, commercial, retail, industrial, and even unique ones like healthcare facilities or timberlands. Each presents its own set of potential returns and risks. Delving into these specifics will guide you towards the type that meshes well with your financial ambitions and risk capacity.

- Step three: Scrutinize the performance of the REIT. While the past isn't a guaranteed predictor of the future, it can furnish useful knowledge. Look out for stable earnings, consistent dividend disbursements, and an adept team at the helm. You can get this information from the annual reports of the REIT or from financial news portals.

- Step four: Pick your investment platform. While some may lean towards the traditional brokerage route, others might find a robo-advisor more convenient. Whatever your preference, there's a suitable platform for you.

- Step five: Take the plunge. But remember, patience is a virtue. Emphasize diversification. Perhaps you'll begin with a modest stake in a healthcare REIT and eventually branch out to a retail or industrial one.

- Step six: Stay on top of your investment. Keep tabs on your REIT's performance and tweak your strategy when necessary. Market trends shift, economies sway, and your financial objectives might change. It's crucial to stay in tune with your investments.

There you have it: The roadmap to start investing in REITs. Remember, every monumental journey begins with a single stride.

Researching REITs

It's time to dive deeper into the crucial task of researching these intriguing investment options. Fear not; it's less about jargon and more about knowing what to look for.

> Kick things off by pinpointing the REITs that fascinate you. Residential, commercial, or niche ones like healthcare facilities—each have unique features.

Understanding these helps identify the ones that match your financial aspirations and risk tolerance.

Now, wear your detective hat. Dive into the REIT's past. While it doesn't dictate the future, it does reveal telling patterns. Look for stable earnings, dividends, and resilience during market turbulence. This information is usually in the annual report or financial news portals.

The next stop? The management team. They are at the helm, steering the ship. Seek seasoned professionals with solid real estate experience. This ensures your investments are in capable hands.

Also, understand the REIT's business strategy. Do they prioritize property acquisitions or value maximization from existing assets? Do they specialize in a particular region or property type? These decisions can influence the REIT's performance.

Finally, keep an eye on overall market trends and economic indicators. These factors can sway all REITs. For instance, low-interest rates often favor REITs as they rely on debt for operations.

And there you have it. Researching REITs isn't as daunting as it first appears. It's all about equipping yourself with the correct information, knowing which inquiries to make, and understanding how to source the answers. This preparation paves the way for a confident venture into REIT investing.

Opening a Brokerage Account

Think of a brokerage account as your personal access point to the world of REITs. It's the space where you'll be buying, maintaining, and selling your REIT shares. So how do you get started with one?

Firstly, find a brokerage account that fits like a glove with your requirements. Traditional brokerages are more comprehensive, providing a full suite of services, including investment counsel. Alternatively, online brokerages tend to have lower fees, which works well for the independent investor.

Next up, it's time to compare different brokerage firms. Pay attention to their commission charges, account minimums, the variety of investment options they offer, their customer service quality, and the overall ease of use of their platforms. This is going to be your financial dashboard, so ensure it's up to par.

After you've picked the brokerage that aligns well with your needs, it's time to get registered. This typically includes completing an online form where you'll need to share some personal information. Details like your name, address, social security number, employment specifics, and a bit about your investment past and aspirations will be asked for.

Next in line is to seed your account with some capital. This is usually as simple as making a transfer from your existing bank account. Be aware of any minimum deposit requirements your chosen brokerage might have. And if a hefty initial deposit isn't feasible for you, that's okay. REITs serve as an inviting entry point into the realm of real estate investing without requiring you to fork out a king's ransom. Once your account is activated and sufficiently funded, you're ready to dive into the world of REIT investing.

However, remember that investing is not a race; it's a long, steady journey. So, take the time you need, and don't allow fleeting market turbulence to derail your long-term financial plan. Stay focused and keep your eyes on your ultimate financial destination (Marquit, 2023).

Buying and Selling REIT Shares

With your brokerage account humming, the exciting part begins—buying and selling REIT shares. You've done the prep, picked your brokerage, and filled out your account. Now, the real action unfolds. Buying REIT shares is as easy as investing in any other public company.

The procedure is straightforward. Access your brokerage account, click on the ticker symbol of the preferred REIT, determine the share quantity, and press the "buy" button. But it's not all about pressing "buy." You need to think about the price, the track record of the REIT, and its prospects for future expansion.

Before you hit that 'buy' button, a few key considerations need your attention. Have your investments been sufficiently diversified? Is your portfolio tilting excessively towards one real estate market segment? Can you stomach the risk tied to the REIT you're eyeing? Keep in mind that every REIT is its own unique entity. Some have a diverse investment portfolio, while others hone in on specific niches.

Turning to selling REIT shares, the procedure is quite similar to buying them, just in reverse. You'll locate the REIT in your portfolio on your brokerage platform, determine the number of shares you wish to sell, and then hit the "sell" button. It sounds easy, doesn't it? But wait, it's not always about hitting "sell" when the prices tumble. It's crucial to understand the reasons behind the price drop. Is it a momentary dip or a signal of a more persistent issue?

The decision to sell should also mesh well with your broader investment strategy. Are you selling because you need the funds, or are you readjusting your portfolio? Are there more lucrative avenues to invest your capital? Or maybe you're just trying to decrease your exposure to the real estate market.

While the act of purchasing and trading REIT shares may seem as simple as hitting "buy" or "sell" there's a well-considered strategy behind each decision. The secret is to stay patient, adhere to your strategy, and ensure every step aligns with your long-term financial aspirations.

Diversifying Your REIT Portfolio

The bedrock of savvy investing is undoubtedly diversification, and this principle holds its weight equally when you're navigating the waters of Real Estate Investment Trusts. Picture diversification as your financial safety helmet, your risk-dampening plan that shields your meticulously accumulated wealth from unpredictable market gusts.

Now, you may wonder, *Why all this hype around diversification?* The world of investing is a sea of uncertainties, and no one holds the secret compass to precisely chart the market's next move. Even REITs that seem to have the Midas touch can experience downturns. Diversification steps in here, acting as your financial life vest, keeping your entire investment portfolio afloat even when one investment seems to be taking on water.

Diversifying a REIT portfolio is like walking a financial tightrope. By distributing your investments across an array of REITs, you're reducing the risk linked to any single one. In simpler terms, if one REIT slips, the others in your portfolio can help balance the fall.

But remember, diversification isn't just about owning multiple REITs. Diversification extends beyond merely spreading your funds across various REITs. It's about nurturing a portfolio that embodies the rich spectrum of the real estate market—from commercial to industrial, residential to healthcare, and everything in between. Each sector dances to its own economic rhythm, and by investing across sectors, you avoid overexposing yourself to one particular dance.

Also, consider the geography of your investments. REITs offer the opportunity to dip your toes into property markets nationwide and even internationally. Different regions have unique market dynamics and growth opportunities, adding yet another dimension of diversification.

However, it's important to remember that while diversification acts as a safety harness during market turbulence, it's not an ironclad guarantee against loss. It's a risk management tool, not a risk eradicator. After all, any investment decision comes with its own slice of risk.

Finally, keep in mind that diversification within your REIT portfolio isn't a task you tick off and then ignore. It's an ongoing commitment, requiring regular check-ins and adjustments to ensure it remains in line with your financial aspirations and risk tolerance zone. As market conditions shift and life circumstances evolve, so should your portfolio.

> Diversification in your REIT portfolio isn't just a good thing to have; it's a must-have. It softens the impact of potential losses, widens your exposure to various market sectors, and helps transform your financial journey from a white-knuckle rollercoaster ride into a more stable uphill trek.

Strategies for Diversifying Within the REIT Market

Diversifying in the REIT market isn't just about casting your lot with different trusts. It goes deeper, requiring a blend of investments across various sectors of the real estate market and even branching out into other asset classes.

Consider the various slices of the real estate pie. There are commercial, residential, industrial, healthcare, retail, and more. Each of these sectors behaves differently under varying market conditions. By spreading your investments across multiple sectors, you're building a safety net against sector-specific downturns.

Don't forget the importance of diversifying across geographies. The dynamics of real estate can shift wildly, whether you're looking at different regions, crossing country borders, or even hopping between continents. By choosing REITs that own properties in a variety of locations, you're adding another layer of protection against localized market declines.

True diversification, however, isn't confined to the real estate landscape. It's also about spreading your risk across different asset classes like bonds, stocks, commodities, and cash. This broad-based diversification can balance out the inherent risk of real estate investments and offer resilience when the market faces a slump.

Remember, diversification isn't a one-time event but an ongoing commitment. As the market ebbs and flows and your financial goals shift, so should your portfolio. Regular portfolio reviews will ensure your investments continue to match your risk tolerance and financial aspirations.

Key Takeaways

- A solid grasp of REITs' composition and operations lays the foundation for a fruitful venture into this investment avenue. Recognize REITs as entities that own, manage, and oversee a wide range of real estate assets, offering you a slice of the real estate market without the usual hassles.

- Delving deep into research is the secret sauce to making it big in REIT investments. This includes investigating the array of REIT types, their associated risks and rewards, and meticulously examining their performance history and managerial competence.

- Your choice of investment vehicle greatly influences your journey into REIT investing. From old-school brokerages to futuristic robo-advisors, you're sure to find an investment platform that fits like a glove with your unique requirements.

- Spreading your eggs across various REIT baskets is a potent risk mitigation strategy. By ensuring your investments span various REIT types and geographical regions, you can secure your financial interests against market fluctuations.

- Keeping a vigilant eye on your REIT portfolio and making necessary adjustments is integral to its success. With market dynamics in constant flux and your financial goals possibly evolving, your investment strategy may need timely tweaks.

Chapter Summary

This chapter ushered you into the exhilarating universe of Real Estate Investment Trusts. Starting from the ground up, it acquainted you with the core structure and functionality of REITs before it led you through the steps to becoming a REIT investor.

It underscored the role of comprehensive research in choosing the right REITs. This includes understanding the different types of REITs, their past performance metrics, and the skills of the management team. It also offered guidance on selecting an investment platform that complements your needs and preferences.

This chapter highlighted the importance of diversification in building a sturdy REIT portfolio. This includes investing across a variety of REITs and maintaining a geographically diverse portfolio to buffer against localized market downturns.

Finally, it reminded you of the need to monitor their investments regularly and make strategic adjustments in response to market trends and changes in financial goals. In essence, this chapter served as a trusted companion for those embarking on their REIT investment journey.

After navigating the fundamentals of investing in REITs, you're now ready for the next level. The following chapter deciphers the critical role metrics play in REIT investing. It's all about the numbers—financial metrics, operational metrics, funds from operations, and more. Prepare to unearth how these pivotal figures can direct your investment approach.

CHAPTER 5

Key Metrics for Investing in REITs

Know what you own, and know why you own it.

–Peter Lynch

Imagine owning the ultimate toolkit that decodes the labyrinth of REIT investing, a tool that reveals hidden opportunities and alerts you to potential hazards. This is the magic of metrics.

Get ready to unlock a universe where figures weave narratives— narratives of prospective returns, measured risks, and data-driven investment choices. This chapter is your key to deciphering the language of these digits—the significance and varied types of REIT metrics. This isn't merely about crunching numbers; it's about comprehending their hidden messages.

You'll traverse through the realms of financial and operational metrics, deciphering the nuances of funds from operations, grasping the role of the Price-to-FFO ratio, and demystifying the principle of Net Asset Value (NAV). On the operational front, you'll grasp the importance of the Occupancy Rate, delve into the nuances of Average Rent per Square Foot, and scrutinize the Operating Expense Ratio.

But this chapter isn't merely a guide to understanding these metrics individually. It's about orchestrating them into a harmonious investment strategy. You'll learn how to interpret these metrics and, more importantly, how to strategically apply them to your REIT investment approach. Remember, it's essential to look at multiple metrics, and knowing how to weigh the trade-off between different metrics could be the key to unlocking lucrative investments. So, strap in for a thrilling journey through the numerical lens of astute REIT investing.

Importance of Metrics in REIT Investing

Metrics in REIT investing are like guiding stars in a vast financial galaxy. They chart the course, assisting you in traversing the universe of investment choices. They're your celestial guide, leading you to the planets of prosperity and helping you circumvent the black holes of risky ventures.

Here's a simple analogy. Imagine each REIT as an intriguing novel. Its cover and synopsis may pique your interest, but the true substance resides within its chapters. Analogously, the real narrative of a REIT unfolds through its metrics. These numbers unlock insights into the trust's operations, its financial stability, and the likelihood of future returns. A cursory look won't do justice; you have to dive in, scrutinize, and draw meaningful comparisons.

In a nutshell, these metrics, when viewed collectively, sketch a comprehensive portrait of the REIT's performance, potential returns, and associated risks. They empower investors to compare different REITs, identify growth opportunities, and pinpoint potential red flags.

However, it's crucial to remember that these metrics aren't predictive magic wands. They don't foretell the future. Rather, they're instruments that, when wielded correctly, can assist in making informed decisions. Also, it's vital to comprehend that each metric narrates just a fragment of the story. Hence, considering a range of metrics simultaneously is key to achieving a well-rounded perspective.

Different Types of REIT Metrics

Using your mind's eye, visualize finding yourself on the threshold of unfamiliar territory. The language you need to master? Metrics. That's right; metrics are the secret code that, once deciphered, can lead to successful Real Estate Investment Trust investing.

Financial metrics—those are the big players in the game. Picture Funds from Operations (FFO) as a snapshot of a REIT's performance. It's a measure of net income, but with a few adjustments—adding back in depreciation and amortization and excluding profits from property sales. This offers a more precise view of how the REIT is functioning operationally.

Then there's the Price-to-FFO ratio, a bit like a distant cousin to the Price-to-Earnings ratio used in other stock evaluations. This ratio serves as a tool to weigh the valuation of the REIT against its earnings. Also, in this clan of financial metrics, we have the Net Asset Value. It's the total value of a REIT's real estate assets after subtracting any liabilities. It's a handy metric for figuring out if a REIT might be undervalued or overvalued on the market.

Now, let's switch gears to operational metrics. These give a sneak peek into how the REIT's properties are performing. Occupancy Rate, for example, is a key player. It shows the portion of the REIT's properties that are currently leased. A higher occupancy rate usually spells good news. Then there's the Average Rent per Square Foot. This metric offers valuable insights into the income the REIT is accruing from its properties.

And don't forget the Operating Expense Ratio. This metric weighs the costs of managing the REIT's properties against its total revenue. Lower ratios tend to indicate that the REIT is operating efficiently.

But remember, these metrics aren't meant to stand alone. They're like individual colors on a palette—it's the combination that creates the final masterpiece. Let's discuss them individually and at length below (CFI Team, 2023b).

Financial Metrics

We've already had a brief introduction to FFOs, the Price-to-FFO ratio, and the Net Asset Value. Now, let's delve into their significance and their role in evaluating a REIT.

> By incorporating specific adjustments to net income—like adding back depreciation and amortization and excluding any property sales profits or losses—it provides a clear lens into the operational efficiency of the trust.

Then, the Price-to-FFO ratio comes into play. It's similar to the Price-to-Earnings ratio used in traditional stock evaluations but tailored for REITs using the FFO. This metric serves as your north star, steering you towards potentially undervalued investment opportunities.

Let's not forget the Net Asset Value. This metric mirrors a REIT's financial statement, representing the total value of its real estate assets after liabilities have been deducted. It provides a snapshot of the intrinsic asset value of a REIT, offering insights into whether the trust is overvalued or undervalued in the market.

Operational Metrics

Alright, let's dive right into the heart of these operational metrics, starting with Occupancy Rate—a term you'll stumble upon quite frequently.

This metric is a numerical representation of the percentage of a REIT's properties that are currently leased. If a REIT has an occupancy rate of 95%, that means 95% of its properties are currently rented out. This is usually a positive sign because it means the properties are in demand, which in turn ensures regular rental income for the REIT. Yet, it's essential to keep tabs on this figure over time, as sudden drops could signal trouble—like tenants leaving due to increasing rents or a location becoming less desirable.

Next in line is the Average Rent per Square Foot. This figure is the average amount of rent the REIT collects for each square foot of its leasable property. It provides a clear picture of the income potential of the REIT's portfolio. Take, for example, a REIT showcasing a high Average Rent per Square Foot. This generally implies the properties lie within areas high in demand, locations where tenants don't mind shelling out an extra dime for their spaces. However, a sudden dip in this figure could indicate tenants bargaining for lower rents or a shift in the tenant mix towards those who pay less per square foot.

Last but definitely not least is the Operating Expense Ratio. This metric is a measure of the cost of operating the REIT's properties compared to its total income. It's expressed as a percentage. For example, if a REIT has an Operating Expense Ratio of 30%, this means it spends 30 cents to earn every dollar in revenue. A lower ratio generally suggests that a REIT is being run efficiently, keeping more of its income as profit. A sudden increase in this ratio could signal that the REIT's costs are rising faster than its income, which could squeeze profits.

Think of these financial metrics as the secret sauce of your investment strategy. Each one narrates a segment of the story, and when combined, they offer a more complete narrative. They equip you with the knowledge to evaluate a REIT's financial standing, profitability, and valuation, guiding your investment decisions.

Explanation of How to Use REIT Metrics in Investment Strategy

With a good handle on the crucial role of metrics in REIT investing and a solid understanding of the various types of REIT metrics, it's time to up the game. Let's move on to how to effectively wield these metrics as part of your strategic investment approach.

Start with Funds From Operations. When you notice a REIT with a steadily increasing FFO, it may signal that the company is making wise property investments and effectively managing its expenses. This can be a positive indicator of potential investment.

Take the example of REIT 'A.' If you see that A has increased its FFO consistently over the past five years, it might suggest that A's management is effectively generating profits from its operations. This could make 'A' a strong contender for your investment dollars.

Next, consider the Price-to-FFO ratio. Let's say REIT 'A' has a lower Price-to-FFO ratio compared to other REITs in the same sector. This might suggest that A is undervalued, offering an opportunity for you to potentially buy shares at a discount.

Wrapping things up, let's turn the spotlight on Dividend Yield. Remember how the unique structure of REITs demands that they distribute a certain percentage of their income to shareholders? This often leads to higher dividend yields, setting REITs apart from many other stock categories. A high dividend yield can be enticing, but it's essential to investigate the reason behind the high yield. It could be a sign of financial instability, or it could indicate a strong, profitable REIT that is returning substantial earnings to shareholders.

For instance, if REIT 'A' has a high dividend yield but its FFO is decreasing, it might be a warning sign of financial trouble. Conversely, if A's FFO is increasing alongside a high yield, it may suggest that A is both profitable and generous in sharing those profits with shareholders.

Analysis of How to Evaluate the Trade-Off Between Different Metrics

Imagine encountering a REIT with a high FFO, signaling strong operational profitability. Yet, this very same REIT might have a subdued Dividend Yield, denoting a less substantial income return. Here's a quandary: Which metric should carry more weight in your investment decisions?

This is where the finesse of evaluating trade-offs takes the spotlight. If your investment strategy is anchored on generating a consistent income stream, a robust Dividend Yield might be more appealing. However, if your focus lies on the operational strength and profitability of a REIT, a high FFO might hold more sway

Consider adding a new dimension to your view by bringing the Debt-to-Equity ratio into focus. This ratio, a useful tool in the investor's kit, gauges a business' financial leverage. A REIT could boast a high FFO, indicative of impressive operational profitability, but also present a high Debt-to-Equity ratio, signaling a higher financial risk.

Your choice here may hinge on your risk tolerance. If you're the cautious type, a REIT with a lower Debt-to-Equity ratio might feel more comfortable, even if it means accepting a lower FFO. Alternatively, if you're comfortable with more risk for potentially larger returns, a REIT with a high FFO might be more to your liking. And let's not forget the Price-to-FFO ratio, a REIT-specific adaptation of the classic Price-to-Earnings ratio. This metric can offer additional insight into whether a REIT is undervalued or overpriced, adding another facet to your investment decision-making process.

Key Takeaways

- Cracking the code of metrics is the name of the game in REIT investing, offering investors the ability to discern the strengths and weaknesses of different trusts.

- With financial metrics like Funds from Operations, Price-to-FFO ratio, and Net Asset Value in your toolbox, you're ready to navigate the economic labyrinth of a REIT.

  Operational metrics are your flashlight in the dark, revealing the state of a REIT's property management, including Occupancy Rate, Average Rent per Square Foot, and Operating Expense Ratio.

- Spotting a rising FFO and a sensible Price-to-FFO ratio is like finding a treasure map, pointing you towards potentially profitable REITs.

- Juggling different metrics and comprehending the trade-offs between them is the art of REIT investing, requiring alignment with your personal investment strategy and risk comfort zone.

Chapter Summary

The passage highlights the fundamental role metrics play in REIT investing. The trio of financial metrics—FFO, Price-to-FFO ratio, and NAV—serve as your compass, pointing out the fiscal health of a REIT. Operational metrics, meanwhile, shed light on the effectiveness of a REIT's property management. Recognizing a REIT with a steady FFO rise and a balanced Price-to-FFO ratio can lead to a profitable investment. But remember, mastering these metrics and knowing how to weigh them against each other is a personalized dance, with steps dictated by your unique investment objectives and risk threshold.

Eager to expand your investing savvy? In the next chapter, we'll be discussing more of the stuff that really makes a difference in your investment journey, such as understanding financial statements and weighing dividends and yields. Let's get this show on the road and fine-tune your investment strategy.

CHAPTER 6

Evaluating REITs

Know what you own, and know why you own it.

–Peter Lynch

Let's say you're eyeing a new smartphone. Would you just rush to the checkout, or would you explore its features, compare prices, and check user reviews first? It's a no-brainer, right? The same prudence applies when investing in Real Estate Investment Trusts.

In this chapter, we'll learn to navigate the intricacies of REIT financial statements. You'll decode the mysteries of balance sheets, income statements, and cash flow statements!

You'll also uncover the secret sauce that makes REITs so enticing: dividends and yields. You'll learn to evaluate these income engines and how they stack up against other income-generating investments.

Prepare for enlightenment!

Understanding REIT Financial Statements

Consider financial statements as treasure maps, leading you to insights about a company's financial health and future prospects. For REITs, these maps are crucial for enlightened investment decisions—the tools you need? A keen eye for balance sheets, income statements, and cash flow statements.

See the balance sheet as a comprehensive photo album of a REIT's financial condition at a specific moment. It gives you a bird's-eye view of the REIT's assets (properties it owns and profits from), liabilities (obligations such as loans for property purchases), and shareholders' equity (the part of the company that belongs to shareholders). Equity is what remains after liabilities are separated from assets.

Next on our itinerary is the income statement, also known as the profit and loss statement. It's a vibrant timeline of a REIT's revenues and expenses over a certain period. This statement provides a transparent view of the REIT's profitability by displaying earnings, expenditures, and the resulting net income.

Don't forget about the cash flow statement, the unsung hero of financial analysis. It monitors the cash entering and leaving through three fundamental business activities: operations, investing, and financing. This statement unveils the REIT's capacity to generate cash, which is essential for sustaining operations, distributing dividends, and fueling future growth.

Decoding REIT financial statements might feel like mastering a new language. However, once you get the hang of it, you'll be capable of identifying a financially robust REIT, steering clear of potential pitfalls, and making wiser decisions about your investments (Harper, 2022).

Interpreting REIT Financial Statements

The first document you'll encounter is the Balance Sheet. This document gives you a clear picture of a REIT's assets, liabilities, and shareholder's equity at a specific point in time. Assets are anything the REIT owns that holds value, such as properties and other investments. Liabilities refer to the REIT's obligations, like loans and other debts. The difference between assets and liabilities reveals the shareholders' equity, a measure of the REIT's net worth.

Then there's the Income Statement. This document shows you the REIT's revenue, costs, and net income over a set period, typically a quarter or a year. It gives insights into the REIT's profitability and how well it generates income from its operations.

Next up is the Cash Flow Statement. It provides a detailed account of the REIT's cash inflows and outflows. Positive cash flow from operating activities is a promising sign, indicating that the REIT is generating sufficient cash from its main business activities.

Each statement provides a different perspective on the REIT's financial health. Together, they give a comprehensive view, much like different angles of a sculpture give a complete view of the artwork.

Take the Balance Sheet, for example. A high ratio of liabilities to assets could imply a heavy debt burden. However, this might not be alarming if the Income Statement demonstrates robust and consistent revenue, indicating the REIT can comfortably service its debts.

By developing the ability to read and interpret REIT financial statements, you're equipping yourself with the tools needed to win as an investor.

Key Takeaways

- Mastering REIT financial statements is a must-have skill for any savvy investor.

- A balance sheet serves as your lens into the financial health of a REIT at a particular moment in time.

- The income statement tells the story of a REIT's profitability journey over a given timeframe.

- The cash flow statement is your crystal ball into the REIT's potential for generating cash, a key indicator of its future growth and dividend distribution capacity.

- The more fluent you become in interpreting these financial statements, the better equipped you are to spot a solid REIT investment and sidestep potential financial landmines.

Chapter Summary

The spotlight of the excerpt is on the pivotal role that REIT financial statements play in making sharp investment decisions.

The three key financial documents—balance sheets, income statements, and cash flow statements—are likened to different facets of a REIT's financial persona. Balance sheets offer a picture of the REIT's net worth; income statements outline its capacity to turn a profit, and cash flow statements offer insight into its cash-generating abilities. A holistic understanding of these documents provides a 360-degree view of a REIT's financial well-being, empowering investors to identify promising opportunities and evade possible hazards. Ultimately, the piece drives home the message that the ability to read and interpret REIT financial statements is like having a secret weapon in your investment arsenal.

Now that we've unraveled REIT financial statements let's turn the page to a thrilling topic. We're about to discuss market risks, swings in interest rates, and the challenges of operations. But hold tight, because we'll also discover the rewards and strategies to manage these risks, making REITs a compelling investment ride.

CHAPTER 7

REIT Risks and Rewards

Do not be embarrassed by your failures, learn from them and start again.

–Richard Branson

Think of REIT investing as the thrill of riding a rollercoaster. The anticipation as you approach the peaks, the butterflies as you plummet into the troughs—yet, just as you'd want to know the safety measures of the rollercoaster, it's important to understand the risks and rewards associated with investing in REITs.

Like any thrilling ride, REIT investing is not without its ups and downs. Market fluctuations, interest rate changes, and operational challenges can all impact your journey. But fear not; this chapter is your trusted guide, ready to help you navigate the real estate market's rollercoaster with strategies to manage risks and harness rewards. In the heart of this chapter, you'll uncover more about the art of portfolio diversification, understand why keeping a keen eye on your investments is paramount, and why it might be smart to peek into the world of alternative investments.

Risks Associated With Investing in REITs

While the road less traveled by REIT investors can lead to enticing rewards, it's crucial to familiarize yourself with potential risks. This chapter serves as your guide to navigating the potential pitfalls of REIT investing, equipping you to take each step with confidence and knowledge.

> Let's kick things off by exploring the real estate market's risks. Real estate, like any investment, isn't immune to market volatility. Elements such as economic climate, job market strength, and societal trends can sway property values and rental income.

A REIT investment means placing your hard-earned money into properties that might be influenced by these external dynamics. It's important to remember that each real estate sector responds differently to these factors, so understanding the specific domain in which a REIT operates is key. For instance, a REIT that primarily invests in retail spaces might be more sensitive to shifts in consumer spending.

Interest rate risk also deserves our attention. As interest rates climb, borrowing becomes more expensive, which can increase the cost for REITs to secure property acquisitions and refinance existing debt. Additionally, rising interest rates can create ripples across the wider investment environment, potentially making other assets more appealing than REITs. This shift in investor focus can drive REIT share prices down and make dividend yields less competitive. Keeping tabs on interest rate trends and considering their potential impact on your REIT investments is a smart move.

> Operational risk is another factor that requires careful consideration. This risk encompasses the potential obstacles a REIT may encounter in property management or strategy execution.

Challenges such as frequent tenant turnover, vacant properties, or unforeseen maintenance expenses can negatively impact the REIT's cash flow and, consequently, its ability to distribute dividends. To evaluate operational risk, examine the REIT's performance history, the competence of its management team, and the quality of its property portfolio.

Investing in REITs can be an enriching journey, but understanding the potential risks is a must. With awareness of these risks and the right strategies to manage them, you'll be equipped to traverse the REIT landscape and make sound financial decisions for your future.

How to Manage REIT Risks

Like any investment, REITs come with their own unique blend of risks. A repertoire of risk management strategies can bolster the chance that your investment journey will leave you with a delightful aftertaste.

1. **Navigating the REIT Terrain**: Embarking on a REIT's journey without comprehending the landscape is like setting off on a voyage with no compass. REITs come in three varieties: equity, mortgage, and hybrid. Each carries its own distinct risk profile, and

understanding these nuances can bolster your investment confidence.

Equity REITs, proprietors, and overseers of properties, typically face market risks such as wavering property values and occupancy rates. Mortgage REITs, investors in mortgages or mortgage-backed securities, react more sharply to interest rate shifts. Hybrid REITs, a cocktail of both, bring together these risks.

2. **The art of diversification**: Diversification, a time-honored risk management technique, rings true for REITs as well. Distributing investments across an assortment of REITs can effectively manage risk. Consider a blend of different REIT types (equity, mortgage, hybrid) and various sectors such as residential, retail, healthcare, or industrial properties. Diversification can cushion your portfolio against the blow of a downturn in a single sector.

3. **Regular surveillance and rebalancing**: Even with well-thought-out investment choices under your belt, it's essential to stay vigilant and continually monitor the performance of your REITs. Are market or regulatory shifts likely to have an impact? Regular monitoring can help flag potential issues early, and rebalancing your portfolio can maintain the desired risk level.

4. **Evaluating the management team**: Behind every triumphant REIT is an adept management team. Examine the track record of the team managing the

REIT. Have they consistently made judicious investment decisions? A team armed with experience, expertise, and a robust strategy can significantly enhance the REIT's success and, subsequently, your investment returns.

5. **Decoding the impact of interest rates**: Interest rates can substantially sway REITs, particularly mortgage REITs. Rising interest rates can inflate borrowing costs, potentially squeezing profit margins for REITs and making them less appealing to investors. Decoding the impact of interest rates on your REIT investments can help you foresee changes and tweak your strategy in stride.

6. **Responsiveness to economic conditions**: The real estate industry is delicately tuned to economic conditions. In economic downturns, property values may dip, and occupancy rates may dwindle, affecting REITs' profitability. Understanding this responsiveness and keeping tabs on economic indicators can help you manage this risk.

7. **Evaluate the REIT debt level**: The debt level of a REIT can be a crucial factor in its ability to weather economic storms. A REIT with a high debt level may be more vulnerable to fluctuations in interest rates or downturns in the property market. Scrutinizing the debt-to-equity ratio can reveal a REIT's financial well-being and aid in crafting a sounder investment choice.

8. **Take into account property locations**: That age-old real estate mantra—triple "location"—rings just as true when you're diving into the realm of REITs. The regions and markets in which a REIT's properties are located can significantly impact its performance. For example, a REIT with properties in economically stable regions may offer less risk than one in areas prone to economic volatility.

9. **Examine the quality of properties**: The type and quality of the properties within a REIT's portfolio can also influence its risk level. A REIT with modern, well-maintained properties may have a better chance of attracting and retaining tenants than one with outdated, neglected buildings. This could translate into more stable rental income and, ultimately, dividends for you.

10. **Stay on top of REIT news and trends**: The real estate and REIT markets are dynamic, shaped by various factors such as regulatory changes, market trends, and technological advancements. Keeping yourself updated with the latest news can help you understand the forces driving the REIT market and make timely adjustments to your investment strategy.

Note that while risk management is crucial, your investments should harmonize with your broader financial goals and risk tolerance. Investing in REITs, like any investment, necessitates due diligence, understanding, and monitoring. So, don your financial gourmet hat, equip yourself with these strategies, and concoct a REIT strategy that resonates with your investment taste buds!

Rewards of Investing in REITs

Imagine donning the hat of a real estate titan. How thrilling! Now peel back the curtain of glamor and peek at the backstage: Property management, upkeep issues, untimely tenant calls, and intricate legal matters. Suddenly, the charm fades, doesn't it? But suppose there's a route to real estate investment that bypasses these speed bumps?

REITs are essentially corporations that own or finance revenue-generating real estate, making it possible for individual investors to buy shares in commercial real estate portfolios. A helpful analogy would be to consider them the mutual funds of real estate—a less intimidating entry point into the property market without the landlord label.

What's the draw of REITs? Well, they offer a roster of potential perks for you, the investor. Plus, understanding them is as straightforward as your go-to takeout order.

Dividend Income

Let's kick off with the crowd-pleaser of the REIT world: dividends. REITs give out a large portion of their taxable income as dividends. This often leads to higher dividend yields relative to other stocks, rendering them a magnet for investors seeking income. Think of it as a cascade of cash flowing your way. It sounds appealing, doesn't it?

Diversification

Ever heard the advice, "Avoid keeping all your eggs in one basket?" It's sage counsel for your finances. By channeling funds into REITs, you can scatter your investment across multiple real estate types—retail, residential, healthcare, and beyond. This diversification can dilute risk because who needs extra financial headaches in life?

Liquidity

Have you attempted to offload a house promptly? It often takes way more time than hoped for. With REITs, you dodge this hurdle. REITs are listed on major stock exchanges, meaning shares can be bought or sold as effortlessly as any other publicly-traded stock. Its financial agility is at its peak.

Inflation Hedging

A little nugget of knowledge: Real estate rents and values usually rise with inflation. Thus, REITs could potentially act as a shield against inflation. While there are few guarantees in life, it's comforting to know your investments stand a decent chance against inflation's claws.

Accessibility

Ever felt the real estate market is a bit like an elite party where only the big spenders get an invite? Here's the silver lining: REITs extend a warm welcome to all investors, not merely the ones boasting hefty bank balances. The entry ticket to REITs isn't as wallet-draining as conventional real estate, making it a fairer choice for those yearning to step into the world of property investment.

Expert Management

With REITs, investing in real estate comes with a bonus: a professional management team. These specialists are dedicated to optimizing return on investment, which could mean a plumper income for you. It's a win-win: You invest and reap the benefits without having to lift a finger in property management.

Tax Perks

The structural design of REITs can serve up some tasty tax benefits. Even though dividends are taxed, REITs themselves dodge corporate income tax on profits shared with shareholders. This characteristic helps sidestep the 'double taxation' that other corporations often face.

Proven Track Record

If history is our teacher, then REITs have been star students in the financial world. Over time, REITs have shown robust performance, frequently outperforming traditional stocks and bonds. Although past achievements don't guarantee future victories, REITs' consistency is a testament to their staying power.

Ownership of Tangible Assets

REITs denote ownership in real, physical assets—properties

that hold inherent value. In contrast to some investments that are strictly financial instruments, the assets tied to REITs are unlikely to bottom out. It's comforting to know your investment is anchored in something solid.

Ties to Economic Growth

Real estate typically rides the wave of economic growth, which can result in heightened property demand, increased rents, and higher occupancy rates. By placing your bet on REITs, you stand a chance to benefit from overall economic progress. It's like cruising along the economic highway with your investments in the passenger seat.

Bear in mind that no investment comes risk-free, and REITs are not immune to this rule. As with any stock, the value of a REIT can ascend or descend. Income from REITs may also vary. However, grasping these potential benefits and risks paves the way for an educated decision.

Key Takeaways

- Different flavors of REITs (equity, mortgage, and hybrid) carry unique risk profiles; knowing these subtleties can boost your investing game.

- Sprinkling your investments across a variety of REIT types and sectors is an age-old recipe for risk management.

- Keeping a close eye on your REIT portfolio, along with a keen study of the management team's track record, are vital ingredients for a winning investment strategy.

- Economic cues, interest rates, and a REIT's debt quotient are like puzzle pieces that, when put together, can help you navigate your investment journey more smoothly.

  Staying informed about the latest REIT happenings and studying the quality and locations of properties in a REIT's portfolio can be your secret sauce for investment success.

Chapter Summary

Embarking on the REIT investment journey is a mix of excitement and caution. This chapter introduces you to the potential speed bumps, including market fluctuations, interest rate adjustments, and operational challenges, and offers a roadmap to navigate around them. It emphasizes the importance of understanding the unique characteristics of different REIT types, spreading your investments across various sectors, and staying alert to changes in your REIT portfolio. It also shines a light on the need to dig into the track record of a REIT's management team and scrutinize its debt levels. Furthermore, it underscores the relevance of economic indicators, the quality and location of properties, and the latest REIT trends in shaping your investment decisions. On the flip side, it brings to light the attractive perks of investing in REITs, such as steady income flow, risk dilution, swift transactions, protection against inflation, and more. This chapter culminates by reminding you that investing is a blend of risks and rewards, and a well-informed decision can be your best bet on the investment table.

The next chapter beckons you to roll up your sleeves and discover the art of crafting a stellar REIT portfolio. We're going to traverse the landscape of sectors and geographies, learn the rhythm of routine checks and rebalances, and unwrap the mystery of REIT ETFs. Onward to the next leg of this financial expedition!

CHAPTER 8

REITs and Real Estate Investment Strategies

Every person who invests in well-selected real estate in a growing section of a prosperous community adopts the surest and safest method of becoming independent, for real estate is the basis of wealth.

–Theodore Roosevelt

This chapter is all about learning to construct a well-rounded REIT portfolio. You'll uncover the key steps, understand how to diversify across sectors and regions, and know why it's essential to monitor your investments and rebalance when necessary.

We'll analyze real-life examples, like Digital Realty Trust (DLR), with its strong position in the growing data center market, and Ventas (VTR) in the healthcare sector. Conversely, we'll also explore why some REITs, like Washington Prime Group, might warrant a cautious approach due to factors like high debt loads and diminishing mall traffic.

Next, we'll tackle REIT ETFs, breaking down their benefits, such as ease of trading and diversification, while also acknowledging potential disadvantages. By the end of this chapter, you'll be well-equipped to navigate the dynamic world of REIT investing with newfound confidence.

Building a REIT Portfolio

Ready to construct a rock-solid REIT portfolio? In this section, we'll consider the steps that will help you build a versatile and resilient REIT portfolio:

1. Diversification Across Sectors: The initial phase of this journey involves comprehending the importance of sector diversification. REITs span various sectors such as residential, healthcare, retail, industrial, and more. Each of these sectors carries unique risks and rewards. For instance, healthcare REITs might offer stability due to long-term leases, while retail REITs could exhibit volatility in response to shifting consumer patterns. Therefore, crafting a balanced portfolio entails including REITs from a variety of sectors, ensuring you're not overly reliant on one type of real estate.

2. Geographical Diversification: Location is a pivotal factor in real estate and, by extension, in REIT investing. Different regions exhibit unique economic dynamics, property demand, and growth potential. Spreading your REIT investments across diverse geographical areas can help cushion the risk associated with any single market. For instance, a commercial REIT in a thriving city like

Austin, Texas, could counterbalance a slower-performing residential REIT in a less bustling locale.

3. Consistent Monitoring: Just as a garden requires regular tending, your REIT investments need consistent attention. Regular reviews of your portfolio are essential to ensuring that your investments are on track. This includes perusing financial reports, staying updated with news affecting the real estate market, and being aware of regulatory changes that could impact your investments.

4. Portfolio Rebalancing: Over time, some REITs in your portfolio might outshine others, causing a shift in your portfolio's original balance. This could inadvertently alter your risk profile or profitability. Rebalancing comes into play here. This process necessitates selling shares from high-performing REITs and augmenting holdings from underperformers, aiming to maintain the desired diversification and risk level. Remember, rebalancing isn't about chasing the stars but about adhering to your investment strategy.

Constructing a portfolio in the REIT industry is a strategic endeavor that requires comprehension, meticulousness, and a hefty dose of patience. With these steps, you're adequately equipped to chart your course through the REIT landscape, making decisions that align with your financial aspirations. It's important to note that each step is integral, and collectively they contribute to the foundation of a robust portfolio.

Spotlight on Potential Investments

One potential candidate for your portfolio could be the Vanguard Real Estate ETF. This fund covers a vast array of commercial real estate sectors, from swanky hotels to buzzing office spaces. It's a smorgasbord of property types, reducing risk and offering broad exposure. Historically, VNQ has delivered reliable returns and boasts minimal fees, making it a go-to for beginners and seasoned investors alike.

Then there's Prologis Inc. (PLD), a REIT with a knack for logistics real estate—warehouses and distribution centers. With the e-commerce explosion, the demand for such spaces is skyrocketing, driving consistent returns and growth potential for PLD.

But not all that glitters is gold in the world of REITs. For example, Retail Opportunity Investments Corp. (ROIC) may seem enticing with its focus on retail spaces in upscale communities. Nonetheless, as e-commerce flourishes and physical stores lose their appeal, the road ahead for ROIC's performance might encounter some bumps.

Similarly, New Senior Investment Group (SNR), specializing in senior housing and assisted living facilities, might seem like a smart bet given the growing senior population. Yet, it's not exactly a breeze. The hefty costs associated with running these facilities and potential fluctuations in government funding add a layer of unpredictability.

When REITs pique your interest, remember to take a step back and evaluate. Favor those with diverse properties in promising industries, and be cautious of those heavily reliant on a single property type or tenant. Consistent earnings and dividend payouts are also important markers of a good investment. But remember, investing is not a surefire win; risk is part of the game.

Your pursuit of financial freedom is yours alone; it is beautifully unique. Whether it's skyscrapers touching the clouds or modest suburban homes, the right REITs can help grow your wealth and get you closer to your goals. Every investment decision is a stepping stone, taken with thoughtful deliberation and sound financial advice.

REIT ETFs

REIT ETFs serves as a basket of REITs, each one a different hue of the real estate rainbow. You're holding a bouquet of diverse properties, stretching from the zenith of city skyscrapers to the industrial warehouses humming with activity and even touching the novel realms of data centers and telecom towers.

Consider the widely respected Vanguard Real Estate ETF (VNQ). This fund houses a multitude of REITs from various sectors, painting a panoramic picture of the real estate industry within a single portfolio.

Then there's the iShares U.S. Real Estate ETF (IYR). The IYR portfolio extends beyond typical REITs to include real estate development and management companies.

But the story doesn't end with general exposure funds. There's a world of specialized REIT ETFs that zoom in on specific sectors. For instance, the Pacer Benchmark Industrial Real Estate SCTR ETF (INDS) spotlights the industrial REIT sector, capitalizing on the booming e-commerce and logistics industries.

Similarly, the Global X SuperDividend REIT ETF (SRET) has a laser focus on REITs delivering high dividends worldwide, making it a magnet for investors seeking a steady income stream.

Peering beyond the U.S., you'll encounter international REIT ETFs like the SPDR Dow Jones International Real Estate ETF (RWX). RWX provides a window to global real estate, adding a layer of geographical diversification to your portfolio.

Understanding the framework of REIT ETFs is key. It's like a Russian nesting doll—the ETFs own shares in several REITs, which in turn own real estate properties. This intricate structure allows the ETF to mirror a broad index of REITs, opening the doors to vast segments of the real estate market (Chen, 2022).

Benefits and Drawbacks of Investing in REIT ETFs

Now that we know what REIT ETFs are, let's consider the advantages and disadvantages of these intriguing funds.

The Advantages

1. Diversification—No Fuss, No Muss: Picture a real estate empire without the property management drama. By venturing into REIT ETFs, you're spreading your

investment across multiple properties and sectors, from plush apartments to buzzing commercial spaces, all tucked neatly into one investment vehicle.

2. The Magic of Passive Income: Imagine a money tree that drops cash while you're busy living life. That's dividends for you. When you nest in a REIT ETF, those dividends flutter into your pocket, creating a continuous income stream to boost your day job earnings or fuel your retirement dreams.

3. Liquid Gold: Unlike a direct real estate investment that can lock up your funds, REIT ETFs offers the freedom to buy and sell shares on your terms. Need to liquidate some assets or change your investment strategy? No worries. There are no property-selling hassles here.

The Disadvantages

1. The Tax Tangle: As much as dividends are the bees' knees, they can complicate your tax situation. REIT ETF income usually gets taxed as ordinary income, which might land you in a higher tax bracket. So, as the passive income rolls in, remember to reserve a portion for your annual dues to Uncle Sam.

2. The Inflation Infliction: Sure, real estate can serve as a buffer against inflation. Certain property types, like shopping malls or commercial spaces, might fall behind inflation if tenants can't keep up with escalating rent. Consequently, your REIT ETF investment might not surge as rapidly as anticipated during inflationary times.

3. Fee Frenzy: Like most investments, REIT ETFs aren't immune to fees. Keep tabs on the expense ratio, the yearly charge that the fund takes to cover operational costs. Don't forget brokerage commissions or trading fees. Even though these costs might seem insignificant, and over time, they can nibble away at your returns.

There you go! Investing in REIT ETFs can offer portfolio diversification, generate passive income, and deliver a slice of the real estate market. Still, remember to consider the potential setbacks and your own financial aspirations before jumping in.

Key Takeaways

- It's all about spreading your eggs in different baskets when you're building a tough-as-nails REIT portfolio. Don't forget to factor in sectors and geography when you're choosing your investments.

- Keep a close eye on your portfolio and be ready to shuffle things around if needed. Your risk tolerance and investment goals should guide you.

- Look before you leap. When you're scouting for potential additions to your portfolio, focus on the consistency of earnings, the variety of properties, and the regularity of dividend payouts.

- Get to know REIT ETFs. These little wonders can be your ticket to a wider real estate landscape, all in one neat package.

- Weigh the pros and cons before taking the plunge into REIT ETFs. While they can diversify your portfolio and create a passive income stream, they can also complicate your tax situation and have potential susceptibility to inflation.

Chapter Summary

This chapter is your roadmap to navigating the intricate world of REIT investing. It's all about crafting a diverse portfolio that spans different sectors and regions, kind of like a real estate globe-trotter. But it doesn't stop at just choosing your investments. Stay vigilant with your investments and embrace the need for occasional adjustments if your portfolio strays from its intended path.

Then, it's time to level up your game by exploring potential investments. But remember, not all that glitters is gold. You'll need to put on your detective hat and dig deeper into the financials and property types before you make your move.

Now, let's talk about REIT ETFs. These financial instruments are like a one-stop shop for diversifying your portfolio. They're chock-full of different REITs, giving you a slice of the entire real estate market. Before you jump headfirst into REIT ETFs, pause to weigh the other side of the coin. Sure, they can generate a nifty stream of passive income, but they may also muddle your tax affairs and aren't fully insulated from inflation's bite.

Keep this in mind: the control is in your hands. It's your financial journey, after all, and the right REITs can help you reach your destination.

Alright, you've got a firm handle on REIT portfolio building. So let's change gears a bit and take a deep dive into the ever-changing world of REIT industry trends, the whizz-bang of new technology shaking things up, and shifting consumer tastes. We'll also navigate the labyrinth of regulatory changes, trot the globe to suss out international markets, and crack the code on the challenges and potentials they present. Plus, we'll tackle the knotty issue of how economic shifts—think interest rates, inflation, even recession—affect REIT performance. Strap in; we're about to broaden our horizons in the global REIT industry.

CHAPTER 9

The Future of REITs

The future belongs to those who believe in the beauty of their dreams.

–Eleanor Roosevelt

Imagine being able to spot the next big thing in the REIT industry, predict how changing economic conditions will sway the market, or even unlock the potential of emerging markets around the globe. Sounds exciting, doesn't it?

In this chapter, we'll uncover what's next in the REIT industry, get to grips with the tech innovations shaking things up, and understand how shifting consumer preferences and regulatory changes are pulling the strings of the global REIT markets.

We're also going to globe-hop across REIT markets worldwide, uncovering their growth potential and how the US sparked a global REIT revolution. Wondered about the turbulent journey of international investing? Fear not; we're breaking it down.

Of course, we can't sidestep the big, weighty topic that's always lurking in the background: Those pesky economic conditions. We'll untangle the web of how interest rates, inflation, and that dreaded 'R' word (recession) can impact your REIT's performance and the broader real estate market.

Industry Trends and Developments

You know better than anyone that the best investment decisions are grounded in understanding the trends in play, right? So, let's unmask the current and emerging trends in the Real Estate Investment Trust industry together.

It's undeniable that this is the era of technology, and the REIT industry is dancing to its rhythm. Advanced tools like AI and big data analytics are transforming the game, offering REITs a crystal ball of sorts to make informed investment choices by studying market trends and forecasting property values. Then there's blockchain, quietly revolutionizing the property transaction process, reducing fraud, and adding transparency. And let's not forget drones—they're no longer just for stunning aerial photos but are now valuable allies in property inspections and surveys. The mantra here is efficiency and smart work.

Also, the trend of consumers opting to rent rather than buy is thriving, and it's not just about homes anymore. It's cars, fashion, and more. This shift energizes different types of REITs in unexpected ways. Take multifamily REITs, for instance, which are experiencing a boom thanks to the urbanization trend. And let's not forget industrial REITs, riding the wave of e-commerce growth and needing more warehouse space.

And what about office and retail REITs, you ask? Well, they're evolving. Yes, remote work and online shopping have dented their growth, but they're bouncing back by reinventing traditional spaces into mixed-use properties, adding a dash of retail, office, and residential spaces to create thriving community spaces. The key here is adaptation, and the ones who adapt will be the winners as consumer preferences continue to evolve.

Lastly, if REITs were a gripping suspense novel, regulations would be the plot twist, always keeping things interesting. Recent shifts in regulations, especially in tax laws, have had a considerable impact on the REIT industry. Some have been favorable, like the U.S.'s 2017 Tax Cuts and Jobs Act, which offered REITs lower corporate tax rates. But the possibility of less-than-favorable changes, like potential tax hikes, always looms large and could affect REIT profitability.

But, just like a suspense novel's protagonist, REITs find ways to navigate these challenges. They're actively engaging with policymakers to shape future legislation that benefits investors and the public alike. It's a dynamic regulatory landscape that adds a dash of unpredictability and excitement to the mix!

Global REIT Markets

Ready to embark on a global exploration of the world's REIT markets? Excellent!

We kick off the journey in North America. Here, REIT markets have reached a stage of maturity, with the U.S. taking the lead. It's the trailblazer who's seen it all and done it all. Its robust regulatory framework and diverse property sectors make it a magnet for investors worldwide. But let's not forget Canada and Mexico. They're catching up, offering unique opportunities, particularly in residential, retail, and industrial real estate.

Next, we voyage to Europe. Here, the REIT landscape is diverse, with each nation displaying its own distinct features. The United Kingdom, France, and Germany are the usual suspects with thriving markets. However, keep an eye out for smaller but dynamic markets like Spain and Belgium. They're making considerable headway in commercial and residential REITs.

Now, we're off to Asia. This region is a treasure trove of potential. Japan shines brightly with the most substantial REIT market in Asia. Yet, markets in countries like Singapore and Hong Kong are also expanding, fueled by proactive government initiatives and rising investor interest. Emerging stars like India and the Philippines are rapidly developing their REIT markets, showing promising potential.

Next, let's make a quick pit stop in Australia. It's a consistent performer in the REIT world, with a well-established market that makes it an attractive destination for investors seeking reliable returns.

Finally, let's cruise to Africa. This continent is just beginning to realize its potential. South Africa is a pioneer with the most mature REIT market on the continent. However, nations like Morocco, Nigeria, and Kenya are showing promising signs with their nascent REIT markets.

So, as you see, the potential of REIT markets globally is a panorama of opportunities. From established markets promising stability and steady returns to burgeoning ones filled with growth potential, there's a wide array for every investor (*Real estate investment trust*, n.d.; Mattson-Teig, 2022).

Investing in Global REITs and Property Companies

Right off the bat, it's essential to understand the primary appeal of global REITs—diversification. Betting on a single country's property market can be a risky game. By directing your funds into global REITs, you gain exposure to the property landscape in various parts of the world, creating a truly international portfolio.

But hold your horses before you take the plunge. It's crucial to evaluate the property markets in the countries where the REITs are located. Look into their economic resilience, real estate laws, and market dynamics. This practice ensures that your investment decisions are well-informed.

> With global REITs, your profit streams from two sources: rental income and capital growth. Imagine receiving a steady income just for holding a stake in these property giants. Additionally, as property values surge, so does the value of your investment.

But like all investments, global REITs carry their own unique set of challenges. Fluctuations in foreign exchange rates, property value shifts, and possible geopolitical disruptions can influence your earnings. That's why a solid understanding of the landscape is key to navigating these risks.

Feeling ready to take the leap? An excellent first step could be investing via an Exchange Traded Fund (ETF) that specializes in global REITs. This approach offers a basket of REITs from various countries, all under the expert care of professional managers.

Alternatively, investing in individual property firms offers another path. This route requires more active management, as you'll need to monitor each company's progress. But it also opens up the possibility for greater returns if you make the right calls.

Remember, the aim isn't to strike gold overnight. The target is to build a resilient, varied portfolio that can withstand turbulence and continue to prosper over time. With careful research, patience, and a sprinkle of audacity, global REITs and property companies can be a lucrative addition to your investment arsenal.

How the U.S. REIT Revolution Spread Around the Globe

A Real Estate Investment Trust is essentially a mutual fund but for real estate. The U.S. introduced this concept back in 1960 with a clear mission: To level the playing field, enabling the average individual to invest in income-producing real estate, usually the playground of the ultra-rich.

The charm of a REIT is its straightforwardness and effectiveness. These vehicles let you buy a piece of the commercial real estate action, similar to purchasing stock, on an exchange. It's akin to having a small piece of a vast, diverse real estate portfolio. The icing on the cake? They're required to dole out at least 90% of their taxable income to shareholders annually, serving up a steady stream of dividends for investors. Remember?

Back to the global odyssey, the U.S. REIT model became a beacon of success, catching the eye of other countries. The 1990s and early 2000s saw a wave of global REIT adoption, influenced by the U.S. model. Australia jumped on the bandwagon in 1971, with the Netherlands hot on its heels in 1969. By the time we ushered in the new millennium, Europe, Asia, and the Americas had embraced their versions of REITs, each fine-tuned to their unique market conditions.

The propagation of REITs wasn't just about copying a winning formula. It was a move to democratize real estate investment. By adopting the REIT model, these countries opened up opportunities for their citizens to harness the wealth-generating power of property without needing a vault full of gold.

Moreover, the global proliferation of REITs has been a blessing for investors keen to diversify their portfolios beyond their borders. Previously, owning property in places like Tokyo or London meant navigating a labyrinth of foreign laws and parting with a significant chunk of change. But with Japanese or British REITs, you can gain exposure to these markets with just a few shares, all from the comfort of your own home.

However, the global march of REITs hasn't been all sunshine and rainbows. The diverse regulatory landscapes, tax regimes, and real estate markets across countries can create discrepancies in how REITs are managed. That's why it's vital for investors to do their research before venturing into international REITs.

The U.S. REIT revolution has been transformative for the world of real estate investment. It has expanded access to the property market, enhanced transparency, and facilitated cross-border real estate investment. It stands as a testament to how solid financial innovation can transcend borders and foster wealth creation on a global scale.

Emerging Markets and the Challenges of International Investing

Imagine emerging markets as vibrant hubs of potential, replete with untapped opportunities that could transform your financial reality. Yet, here's the interesting part: These very markets are also known for their capricious nature, underscored by their unique unpredictability.

These markets symbolize economies perched on the precipice of remarkable growth. They represent countries yearning to carve out their niche in the global economy. However, while the prospect of stellar returns can be enticing, remember that alongside high reward often lurks high risk.

What makes them risky, you wonder? It's a multifaceted jigsaw. Political instability, economic flux, and evolving regulatory frameworks often define emerging markets. Couple this with issues around liquidity and currency volatility, and it's clear that these markets can pose quite a challenge.

Still, the allure of striking it big remains potent. It's the chance to be part of a significant shift right from the onset. If that 'shift' gains momentum, your investments could soar. But does it make sense to venture into these unexplored arenas? That's your call, based on your comfort with risk, your financial aspirations, and your grit to withstand potential financial turbulence.

"So, how do I venture into these markets?" you query. This is where the magic of international investing unfolds, and it's not as intimidating as it might first appear. A diverse mix of investment alternatives awaits you, ranging from mutual funds to exchange-traded funds, all providing a pathway into the vibrant universe of emerging markets. With the rise of robo-advisors and online trading platforms, integrating some global spice into your portfolio is now quite straightforward.

Still, prudence should be your guiding star. Thorough research before taking the plunge is non-negotiable. Understand the unique risks and challenges that each market poses. The economic and political climates of Brazil, India, and South Africa are incredibly distinct, each offering its own set of eccentricities. Stay abreast of developments and ensure the prospect of high returns doesn't blindside potential hurdles.

> Never downplay the importance of diversification. Spreading investments across different markets and sectors can create a buffer if one area faces a downturn. Also, never lose sight of your overarching financial goals.

Are you gunning for long-term growth, or is a quick turnaround your aim? Your investment strategy should mirror these objectives.

Diving into emerging markets and international investing can feel like a riveting odyssey, complete with its share of surprises. But equipped with comprehensive knowledge, an understanding of the inherent risks, and a sound investment plan, you can brave the high seas and potentially seize the rewards.

Impact of Changing Economic Conditions

REITs open the door to investing in large-scale real estate and are particularly attuned to economic shifts. Why? Let's dissect it.

Interest rates are a critical factor. When they climb, the borrowing overheads for REITs also rise, compressing their profits. Moreover, escalating interest rates can render bonds and other fixed-income investments more appealing, possibly nudging investors to divert funds away from REITs.

Inflation, another key economic indicator, has its part to play. As prices ascend, the expenses associated with property upkeep, from refurbishments to repairs, can inflate. If these increased costs can't be counterbalanced with higher rents, the bottom line for REITs could take a hit.

In a flourishing economy, production levels could surge, driving up profits. However, an economic downturn might pull the rug out from under manufacturing as demand for products shrinks.

During times of economic expansion, people are more likely to splurge on eating out or vacations, spurring success in these areas. But in austere economic conditions, discretionary spending is usually the first casualty, shaking the foundations of businesses in this industry.

The tech industry deserves mention too. Though often regarded as robust, it isn't immune to economic fluctuations. In times of prosperity, businesses and consumers might splurge on the latest gadgets, powering the sector. However, during economic contractions, these purchases may be relegated to the "luxury" category and cut back.

Often labeled as defensive due to its ability to weather economic storms better than most, the healthcare sector is not completely invincible. In a sluggish economy, individuals might delay non-urgent procedures, affecting some healthcare subsectors.

Economic conditions are like an invisible puppeteer, directing the fortunes of REITs and diverse industries. Whether it's the undulations of interest rates, the climb, and descent of inflation, or the overall economic weather, these shifts can determine the trajectory of industries. Therefore, keeping a keen eye on economic indicators and understanding their impact on various sectors is more than just good wisdom—it's a smart strategy.

Key Takeaways

- Don't just view drones, AI, or blockchain as buzzwords. These technologies are revolutionizing the REIT industry, driving efficiency, and improving transaction transparency.

- Traditional office and retail REITs are rebounding despite the rise of remote work and e-commerce. They're innovating, creating mixed-use spaces that cater to evolving consumer preferences.

- The dynamic nature of regulations, particularly tax laws, adds an element of suspense to the REIT narrative. Changes can either be a boon or a bane for the industry, affecting profitability.

- Investing in global REITs offers exposure to various property markets, thus providing portfolio diversification. However, a thorough understanding of local market dynamics is essential.

- Interest rates, inflation, and overall economic conditions can greatly impact the various sectors that REITs invest in. Being cognizant of these economic indicators is crucial.

Chapter Summary

The REIT industry is a vibrant tapestry of trends, opportunities, and challenges. Cutting-edge technologies like AI, big data, and drones are reshaping the sector, offering invaluable tools for analysis, property valuation, and even routine tasks like property inspections. Amid changing consumer preferences towards renting and the rise of e-commerce, REITs are adapting by turning traditional spaces into mixed-use properties, combining retail, office, and residential spaces.

> Regulations, especially tax laws, have a significant influence on the industry. While some changes, like the U.S.'s 2017 Tax Cuts and Jobs Act, have been beneficial, potential tax hikes always pose a risk.

However, REITs are not passive spectators and actively engage with policymakers to shape future legislation.

Global REITs also carry their own unique set of challenges, like fluctuations in foreign exchange rates and possible geopolitical disruptions.

The U.S. REIT model has been a beacon of success, influencing other countries to adopt their versions of REITs and democratizing real estate investment. However, each country's diverse regulatory landscapes, tax regimes, and real estate markets can create discrepancies in how REITs are managed.

> Emerging markets offer a plethora of untapped opportunities, yet their inherent unpredictability means they come with high risks. Diversification can mitigate these risks, as can thorough research and a sound investment strategy that aligns with one's financial goals.

We've untangled the web of REIT intricacies, peeked at the tech revolution within the industry, and considered potential speed bumps on the road. Our next adventure takes us into the realm of real estate development. Along the way, we'll uncover other investment pathways that beckons, like private equity and crowdfunding.

CHAPTER 10

REITs and Real Estate Development

Real estate cannot be lost or stolen, nor can it be carried away. Purchased with common sense, paid for in full, and managed with reasonable care, it is about the safest investment in the world.

–Franklin D. Roosevelt

Ever caught yourself admiring the transformation of an old, rundown warehouse into a trendy apartment complex or the sprouting of a modern office space from an empty lot? Imagine being more than just a spectator but an investor, making these transformations possible. Ready to step behind the scaffolding of real estate development?

Here, we'll dissect the processes involved in acquiring, developing, and selling properties. Far from just being vehicles for passive income, REITs take center stage in property development, offering individual investors a chance to play a part in projects of scale, previously a luxury for the ultra-wealthy.

But hold on; real estate investment doesn't end with traditional paths. We'll also set foot in the territories of private equity and crowdfunding, proving there are a multitude of ways to make your mark in the property market.

Understanding Real Estate Development

At its core, real estate development is about turning daydreams into concrete realities. Imagine a shabby, rundown building turning into a swanky, high-rise condominium or a busy shopping complex. That's the magic real estate developer's weave. They spot potential in the most unlikely places, nurture it, and transform it into a tangible asset.

Kickstarting this journey begins with an acquisition. Scour the market, identify the diamond in the rough, and purchase it. Don't rush this step. Understanding the nuances of the neighborhood, zoning laws, and market trends is crucial. This stage is akin to finding the perfect outfit for a special occasion— you won't pick anything without checking every minute detail.

Having identified your ideal property, the next task is to marshal the necessary financing. Unless you have a hidden treasure, you'll need to attract investors or secure loans. Having a comprehensive business plan is key here. It's your project's roadmap, showing your potential backers how you'll navigate from point A to point B (*A guide to*, n.d.).

Then comes the design and planning phase. Collaborate with architects and planners to give a physical form to your vision. This stage requires you to juggle various elements, from building codes to environmental impact assessments. Like assembling a complex puzzle, every piece must fit perfectly.

With the groundwork in place, the stage is set for tangible progress—actual construction. During this process, it's crucial to stay alert, especially when it comes to the budget and project timeline. Remember, consistency and discipline are vital, just as in any endeavor requiring a long-term commitment.

When the construction phase wraps up, the focus shifts to the property's disposition. This could mean leasing it to tenants or selling it outright. It's indeed a satisfying moment to see the fruits of your labor take shape and start to generate returns. Market the property, draw in tenants or buyers, and witness your dream become a vibrant part of the community.

It's important to remember that real estate development demands sweat, perseverance, and a good dose of patience. But with meticulous planning and unshakeable resolve, it can be a rewarding path to creating lasting value (Litvak, 2021).

The Process of Acquiring, Developing, and Selling Real Estate Properties

The acquisition phase is when you scout for the property that could become your gold mine. It involves a deep dive into market analysis, understanding zoning laws, and learning about the property's surrounding environment. This phase is also about visualizing the potential transformation of the property.

Once you've located your property, it's time to gather the financing. Unless you're sitting on a gold mine, this will likely involve securing funds from a bank or from investors who believe in your project. Here, your business plan becomes your showreel, illustrating your strategy to turn this property into a thriving venture. You're essentially creating an intriguing story to secure your funding.

With financing in place, the stage is set for development. Collaborating with architects and planners, you'll design the property and prepare the site. Remember, it's not only about visual appeal but also about conforming to building codes, environmental regulations, and other legal stipulations. It's like constructing a complicated 3D model where each component must fit seamlessly.

The following development is the construction phase. With your detailed plans ready, it's time to bring in the heavy machinery and start building. During this phase, attentiveness to your budget and timeline is crucial, ensuring that everything progresses as planned. Much like a cross-country cyclist, you need to maintain a consistent speed, ensuring endurance till the end.

Finally, you arrive at the stage of selling or leasing. This is where you unveil your finished project to prospective buyers or tenants. Marketing the property effectively, emphasizing its unique features and benefits, is crucial at this juncture. Just as an artist reveals their masterpiece, you'll be presenting your property in the most attractive light possible.

Navigating the world of real estate might seem intimidating initially, but keep in mind that every expert was once a beginner. It's not about quick returns but about recognizing potential, investing your time and energy, and creating a valuable asset. It's about transforming an overlooked building or empty plot into a dynamic part of the community.

Role of REITs in Real Estate Development

Real Estate Investment Trusts are the invisible hands sculpting our urban landscapes, infusing capital into property markets like a life-giving elixir. This financial injection is a lifeline for construction firms, allowing them to transform architectural sketches into tangible structures. Without REITs, many of these architectural masterpieces might remain confined to the drawing board, never gracing our cities with their presence.

But it's not just about financing. REITs also serve as catalysts for innovation within the realm of real estate development. Their deep pockets, filled to the brim with investor funds, empower them to sponsor state-of-the-art designs and pioneer eco-friendly technologies. They're not merely builders; they're trailblazers, establishing fresh trends and setting elevated standards for the industry.

In addition to shaping new construction, REITs have a knack for urban revival. They invest in the reincarnation of underutilized or faded areas, infusing them with renewed vitality. This urban regeneration not only enhances local infrastructure and escalates property values but also sparks job creation and economic growth, serving as a boon for local communities.

Yet, like any powerful entity, REITs can also pose challenges. Their relentless pursuit of shareholder returns can sometimes fuel overdevelopment in certain locales, which could create property market bubbles and escalate the risk of a downturn. Hence, a critical understanding is necessary. While REITs can indeed paint vibrant and prosperous urban landscapes, they must be judiciously managed to avert any potential destabilization of the property market.

The Advantages and Disadvantages of Partnering With REITs for Development Projects

Starting with the bright side—the benefits of partnering with a REIT—first and foremost, they're financially robust and capable of pouring significant capital into your project. This monetary support can help you surmount any fiscal roadblocks that could otherwise hinder your project's progress.

Additionally, REITs boast an extensive reservoir of expertise and industry contacts. Having maneuvered through the labyrinth of real estate development, their market acumen can be a guiding compass. From deciphering market oscillations to having access to the right network, a REIT alliance can propel your project.

REITs are fundamentally committed to delivering steady dividends for their investors, a goal that might not always align with your project's aspirations. At times, this shareholder-centric approach can result in accelerated development and overconstruction in certain regions. While this may initially seem advantageous, it could inflate a real estate bubble, inducing market volatility.

Moreover, while REITs are resource-rich, they also entail a degree of bureaucracy. Decision-making could be prolonged due to multiple managerial tiers. If your project thrives on speed and decisiveness, this could pose an obstacle.

Finally, associating with a REIT could imply relinquishing some creative autonomy. REITs usually adhere to specific project standards and models, which may not accommodate avant-garde ideas or innovative designs. If you cherish creative liberty, this might be a constraint.

In essence, partnering with a REIT for a development project presents a mixed bag of benefits and challenges. The decision isn't universal but should be tailored to your project's unique demands, your financial position, and your comfort with ceding some control. It's a delicate dance between harnessing a REIT's capital and networks and navigating potential drawbacks. Always remember, it's your project, your dream. Any alliance should serve to fortify that vision.

Alternative Ways to Fund Real Estate Development

Let's set REITs aside for the moment and map out alternative routes to finance your potential ventures. There's no need for a compass or a hiking boot—just an open mind and a willingness to explore:

1. Crowdfunding: The real estate world has embraced crowdfunding, a method often associated with start-ups and artistic endeavors. Platforms such as Fundrise, RealtyMogul, and CrowdStreet enable developers to gather funds from a variety of investors. It's an

innovative approach that democratizes investment and could be the perfect tool in your property development toolkit.

2. Seller Financing: Seller financing offers an unconventional way to purchase property: the seller becomes the lender. In this scenario, the seller receives payments over a period of time agreed upon by both parties, similar to a mortgage from a bank. It's an arrangement that benefits both parties—the seller finds a buyer, and you sidestep traditional banking hassles.

3. Private Lending: Support from personal connections or professional investors can provide a much-needed boost to your real estate aspirations. Known as hard money lenders, these individuals offer short-term loans that may carry higher interest rates than bank loans. However, with prompt repayment and a clear vision, this route can be fruitful.

4. Home Equity Loans and Lines of Credit: If you have substantial equity in your current home, it could be harnessed for your next development. Home equity loans and lines of credit are financial products that can help you tap into that sweet, sweet equity you've built up in your home. However, it's crucial to tread carefully here—any setbacks could put your home at risk.

5. Real Estate Investment Partnerships: Collaborating with like-minded investors can be the key to unlocking success. These partnerships combine resources and expertise, paving the way for ambitious undertakings.

Choose your partners with care—a strong collaboration can make the journey smoother and more enjoyable.

6. Angel Investors and Venture Capital: If your real estate project is groundbreaking with high potential returns, it might attract the attention of angel investors or venture capital firms. These entities are constantly scouting for promising opportunities and can offer significant investment. However, they'll typically expect a share of the business, so be prepared for this trade-off.

7. Government Grants and Incentives: Finally, don't overlook the potential of government grants and incentives. These funding sources can provide substantial support for specific projects or areas. Research to see if your project qualifies for any state, local, or federal programs.

Armed with these diverse funding options for real estate development, you're better equipped to find a solution that suits your unique needs.

Key Takeaways

- The journey of real estate development is like a well-choreographed dance; each step from acquisition to final sale or lease needs your full attention, patience, and self-discipline.

- The silent giants of the real estate world, Real Estate

Investment Trusts, are major players in funding and trendsetting. But remember, their fierce commitment to shareholder returns might tip the scales towards overdevelopment and market turbulence.

- Teaming up with REITs? You'll get a sturdy financial backbone and a trove of industry wisdom. But you might have to share the driver's seat of your project, navigate the maze of bureaucracy, and risk overdevelopment due to their shareholder-focused pursuits.

- Funding your real estate dreams can be an adventure, with pathways like crowdfunding, angel investors, and government grants waiting to be explored.

Chapter Summary

In this chapter, we strolled through the fascinating world of real estate development. It all starts with hunting for a property with potential, securing the funds to transform it, designing, and planning it right, overseeing the construction, and finally unveiling it to tenants or buyers. We highlighted how Real Estate Investment Trusts are instrumental in bringing projects to life, although their intense pursuit of shareholder profits could lead to a potential market imbalance.

We also weighed the pros and cons of joining forces with REITs. The benefits? A solid financial backing and a treasure chest of industry knowledge. The downsides? You may have to deal with red tape, risk overdevelopment, and give up some control over your project.

We touched upon other creative ways you can secure funding for your dream project. From crowdfunding platforms and angel investors to government grants, we covered a spectrum of choices that offer you the flexibility to find what fits your needs best.

At the heart of it all, this chapter stressed a truth often overlooked: Real estate development is more than just turning a quick profit. It's a journey of recognizing potential, pouring in time and passion, and creating an asset that stands the test of time. It's an adventure in transforming an overlooked plot or building into a dynamic piece of the community.

You've now mastered real estate development—high five! But have you ever stopped to ponder the tax maze you'd need to traverse when partnering with REITs? Our next stop is the intimidating yet fascinating world of REIT taxation.

We'll deconstruct this complex topic, turning it into something as clear as your morning coffee. But that's not all—we're going to uncover the tantalizing potential for passive income, and the strategic role REITs can play in your estate planning. You're about to up your game!

CHAPTER 11

Tax Considerations for REIT Investors

In this world, nothing can be said to be certain, except death and taxes.

–Benjamin Franklin

You've made it this far, and I bet you're feeling pretty savvy about REITs by now. But there's this little thing called taxation that we need to tackle. Don't panic! It's just another step in becoming a REIT master.

In this chapter, we're going to unmask the mystery behind REITs and taxation. Getting the hang of this could turn an okay investment into an outstanding one. It's all about mastering the art of money elasticity.

Recall that rush of excitement when the concept of passive income through REITs clicked for the first time? Now, take it a step further. The only thing sweeter than watching your money multiply as you snooze is having more of that dough stick around. This is where understanding taxes comes into play.

When you turn the last page of this chapter, you'll have the knowledge to confidently decide how REITs mesh with your investment portfolio.

Taxation of REITs

REITs boast an attractive benefit: exemption from corporate income tax. This is a privilege that most companies can only aspire to have. However, this privilege has its conditions. REITs, as you know, must hand over at least 90% of their taxable income to shareholders. The trade-off? These dividends are not tax-exempt.

When these dividends are credited to your account, they're typically classified as ordinary income, much like your regular earnings from your day job. Regrettably, they don't enjoy the perk of the often-favored lower capital gains tax rate that many investors seek.

However, REIT dividends can sometimes deviate from the norm. They may be classified as qualified dividends or returns of capital, each with unique tax characteristics. Qualified dividends are taxed at a lower rate, making them a favorable outcome. Conversely, the return on capital is not taxed immediately but reduces your investment's cost basis.

While REITs provide an appealing pathway into the real estate market without necessitating direct property ownership, they introduce a level of tax complexity. Despite the REIT itself enjoying freedom from corporate income tax, the dividends you earn will most likely be taxed at your ordinary income tax rate.

Before you plunge into REIT waters, it's a smart move to have a talk with a tax expert. They can guide you through your taxes and provide clarity on how this investment could impact your broader financial portfolio.

REITs and Passive Income

One of the reasons you'll love REITs for passive income generation is something we've repeated in this book: their impressive dividend distribution. Ultimately, this means a more predictable cash flow for you. It's like having a money tree that keeps on giving without the hassle of maintaining physical property.

REITs provide a smooth entry into the real estate market by allowing you to invest in properties without actually owning them. As publicly-traded stocks, REITs offer the flexibility and liquidity you crave in your investment portfolio. Isn't it amazing how you can effortlessly trade shares just like any other stock? This means you can tweak your financial game plan whenever you want, ensuring you're always on top of your money moves.

> Also, by spreading your risk across various types of properties and geographic locations, you protect your investments from local market fluctuations. It's like having a safety net for your finances, ensuring you're not overly exposed to a single area.

Now, let's revisit the tax implications you should keep in mind as a passive income investor. REIT dividends may be taxed as ordinary income, capital gains, or a return of capital, and each has its own unique considerations.

> Ordinary income is often the most prevalent type of REIT dividend and is taxed at your regular income tax rate. While this rate might be higher than what you'd pay on qualified dividends from other stocks, remember to view tax implications within the context of your overall investment strategy.

When the dividends from your REIT are labeled as capital gains, you're in for a treat. You'll actually benefit from a sweeter tax rate that usually falls somewhere between 0% and 20%, based on how much you earn.

Now, this little tax perk can truly give your investment returns a nice boost. When it comes to returns of capital, you won't be taxed when you get them. Instead, they'll just lower your cost basis for the investment.

Just a heads up, though: This might result in higher capital gains taxes when it's time to sell your shares. So, don't forget to consider this when mapping out your financial game plan.

Estate Planning and REITs

With financial goals set, there's no doubt you're eager to establish a lasting legacy for future generations. Including REITs in your estate planning strategy can help achieve those aims while expanding your investment horizons. Here's how:

- **Diversifying assets**: REITs create a unique avenue for

incorporating real estate into your estate planning without the need for direct property ownership. This approach allows you to spread potential risks and build a stronger financial base for both you and your family.

- **Quick fund access**: It's vital to consider how easily your loved ones can access assets in your estate plan. REITs simplify this process by allowing your family to access funds through shares that can be readily traded on the open market. This ensures your heirs can handle immediate expenses or financial responsibilities.

- **Smooth wealth transfer**: REITs play a key role in estate planning by facilitating a seamless transfer of wealth to your heirs. Allocating a portion of your investment portfolio to REITs ensures your wealth can be easily passed on through shared inheritance. This empowers your heirs to either maintain the shares for ongoing income or sell them to cover expenses, putting them in control of their financial destiny.

- **Long-term growth prospects**: Leaving assets with growth potential is crucial in estate planning. REITs provide exposure to the real estate market, which has a history of consistent growth over time. By adding REITs to your estate plan, you're leaving an investment poised to appreciate in value and supply a steady income stream for years to come.

- **Impactful giving**: If philanthropy is a priority in your estate planning, REITs can play a considerable part in realizing that goal. By donating REIT shares to a charity or establishing a charitable trust, you can make a lasting difference in the causes that matter to you while potentially reaping tax benefits.

REITs' role in estate planning goes beyond providing stable income and tax perks. They contribute to a well-rounded estate plan by fostering asset diversification, ensuring liquidity for heirs, enabling wealth transfer, offering long-term growth potential, and facilitating philanthropic endeavors.

The Potential Benefits and Drawbacks of Using REITs as Part of an Estate Plan

Let's explore the potential advantages and drawbacks of adding REITs to your estate plan.

Pros:

1. Steady income flow: REITs generate a consistent income through dividends, which is an appealing aspect of estate planning. This dependable income source can support your heirs, offering them financial security in your absence.

2. Expert management: Investing in a REIT means placing your trust in a team of professionals who oversee the properties and make decisions for you. This relieves you of property management responsibilities, enabling you to concentrate on other facets of your estate plan.

3. Ease of gifting: REIT shares are relatively simple to transfer to your beneficiaries, making them an appealing

option for gifting. The shares can be transferred through a trust, a will, or even as a living gift during your lifetime.

Drawbacks:

1. Limited control: Although expert management can be advantageous, it also results in reduced control over your investment. You won't have decision-making authority over property acquisitions, disposals, or management, which may not be appealing to some investors.

2. Exposure to market shifts: Since REITs are traded on stock markets, they are subject to market fluctuations. The value of your REIT shares could rise and fall with market trends, potentially affecting your estate plan's overall value.

3. Concentration risk: While REITs provide diversification within the real estate sector, they can also introduce concentration risk if a substantial portion of your portfolio is allocated to this asset class. If the real estate market experiences a downturn, your estate's value could suffer.

Key Takeaways

- Although REITs enjoy corporate income tax exemptions, their dividends are typically taxed as ordinary income.

- Generating passive income through REITs offers steady cash flow and ease of share trading.

- Estate planning can benefit from REITs by diversifying assets and ensuring a seamless transfer of wealth.

- Philanthropic goals can be met through REITs by donating shares or creating a charitable trust.

- Some potential drawbacks of using REITs in estate planning include limited control and susceptibility to market fluctuations.

Chapter Summary

Throughout this chapter, you learned that REITs, while exempt from corporate income tax, generally have dividends subject to ordinary income tax.

> The advantages of using REITs for passive income generation were also examined, focusing on reliable cash flow and the convenience of trading shares.

Furthermore, this chapter delved into the advantages of incorporating REITs into estate planning, highlighting asset diversification, smooth wealth transfer, and the facilitation of charitable giving. Despite the benefits, this chapter also brought attention to the potential downsides of using REITs for estate planning, such as reduced control over investments and sensitivity to market shifts.

Now that you've grasped the ins and outs of REITs in estate planning, let's focus our attention on real estate finance. In the upcoming chapter, you'll unravel the fundamentals of financing, explore diverse funding avenues, and comprehend REITs' role in the landscape. Moreover, we'll shed light on alternative financing methods, including banks, private lenders, and crowdfunding platforms, arming you with the knowledge to navigate your real estate investments confidently.

CHAPTER 12

REITs and Real Estate Finance

Real estate investing, even on a very small scale, remains a tried and true means of building an individual's cash flow and wealth.

–Robert Kiyosaki

Are you prepared to explore and master the techniques of funding property investments?

The real estate realm has consistently proven itself as a dependable path to building wealth, but comprehending the intricacies of real estate finance can be overwhelming. Worry not, aspiring investors! In this chapter, the basics of real estate finance will be unraveled, clarifying the diverse assortment of funding avenues and multiple loan alternatives. Additionally, we'll investigate the function of REITs in real estate finance, scrutinizing the pros and cons of utilizing them as a financing method. To wrap things up, we'll examine alternative financing possibilities, such as banks, private lenders, and crowdfunding platforms.

Understanding Real Estate Finance

Real estate finance encompasses the monetary components of acquiring, developing, and managing properties, whether residential or commercial. A solid understanding of these financial principles is necessary for optimizing investments and confidently navigating the real estate landscape.

Central to real estate finance is the notion of leverage. Leverage involves utilizing borrowed funds to finance a real estate investment, anticipating that the property's appreciation will surpass the cost of borrowing. By leveraging other people's capital, investors can potentially magnify their returns and own several properties with a limited personal investment.

A vital aspect of real estate finance is grasping the time value of money. This helps in determining the present value of future cash flows and assessing investment opportunities.

Another essential aspect of real estate finance involves navigating the risk-reward equilibrium. This balancing act requires weighing the prospective profits of an investment against the possible drawbacks.

In real estate, investments with greater risk might offer higher returns, whereas those with lower risk typically result in modest gains. Striking the optimal balance in this risk-reward dynamic is vital for building a prosperous real estate investment portfolio.

Cash flow is a fundamental factor in real estate finance. It pertains to the funds generated from rental income and other sources after subtracting the expenses associated with property management, maintenance, and mortgage payments.

Positive cash flow indicates an investment property generates more income than expenses, while negative cash flow implies the property is costing the investor.

Sources of Funding for Real Estate Projects

Embarking on a real estate project requires adequate funding, and while REITs are one option, there are various other avenues to consider. We discussed some methods in Chapter 10 of this book, so let's examine other solutions. These alternatives can help tailor a financial solution that meets the specific requirements of any venture.

- Real Estate Syndication: This method involves investors pooling their resources to invest in large-scale properties that would be difficult to afford individually. A knowledgeable sponsor manages the property on behalf of investors, who receive a share of profits relative to their investment.

- Self-Directed IRAs: This type of Individual Retirement Account permits using retirement funds for alternative investments like real estate. By leveraging SDIRA, investors can diversify their portfolios and potentially realize higher returns. However, it's crucial to adhere to strict IRS guidelines to avoid penalties.

- Real Estate Investment Clubs: Joining such clubs, whether local or online, connects investors with others, enabling knowledge-sharing and collaboration on investment opportunities. Clubs typically comprise experienced investors, brokers, and property managers, providing valuable insights and networking opportunities.

- Bridge Loans: These short-term financing solutions facilitate property acquisitions before securing long-term financing. Although they come with higher interest rates, bridge loans provide flexibility for time-sensitive opportunities or when funds are needed to bridge the gap between selling and buying properties.

- Commercial Mortgage-Backed Securities (CMBS): CMBS are mortgage-backed securities comprising commercial property loans. They offer investors access to real estate debt investments with relatively lower risk due to diversified loan pools. Developers can access funds via CMBS loans, which are generally more flexible than traditional bank loans.

- Mezzanine Financing: This marriage of debt and equity financing fills the gap between primary financing and developer equity. Mezzanine lenders supply additional funds for a project and receive a higher interest rate than senior lenders, along with potential property equity.

- Joint Ventures: Here, multiple parties cooperate, sharing resources, expertise, and risks to achieve a common goal, such as a real estate development project. Partners contribute capital, skills, or assets and agree on responsibilities, profit-sharing, and exit strategies. This arrangement can benefit all involved, as it distributes risk and combines complementary strengths.

By examining these various funding sources for real estate projects, investors can identify the most appropriate option for their specific needs and goals. These alternatives offer flexibility and growth opportunities, empowering investors to build a strong and successful real estate portfolio.

Different Types of Real Estate Loans

Navigating the property investment landscape requires a solid understanding of the diverse real estate loan options available. These common loan types can help guide your investment journey.

- Conventional Loans: These standard loans, offered by banks and traditional financial institutions, typically necessitate good credit and a substantial down payment.

- Bridge Loans: Also known as "gap" or "interim financing," bridge loans are short-term solutions that assist buyers in managing the transition between purchasing a new property and selling an existing one. Although they can be helpful in fast-paced, competitive markets, they usually come with higher interest rates and fees.

- Commercial Real Estate Loans: Intended for the

acquisition, renovation, or construction of commercial properties like offices, retail spaces, and apartment buildings, these loans have more stringent eligibility requirements, larger down payments, and elevated interest rates compared to residential loans.

- Hard Money Loans: Issued by private investors or companies, hard money loans are short-term financing options for real estate projects. While they carry higher interest rates and shorter repayment periods, they're often easier to qualify for, making them popular among fix-and-flip investors or those with credit difficulties.

- Construction Loans: These loans are specifically designed to fund the building of new properties or the extensive renovation of existing ones. They generally involve interest-only payments during the construction phase and convert to a traditional mortgage once the project is complete.

- Home Equity Loans and Lines of Credit (HELOCs): These financing options allow homeowners to borrow against their property's equity. Home equity loans provide a lump sum at a fixed interest rate, while HELOCs function more like credit cards, enabling borrowers to draw funds as needed with variable interest rates.

- Reverse Mortgages: Aimed at senior homeowners aged 62 and older, reverse mortgages transform a portion of home equity into cash. The loan is repaid when the homeowner sells the property, moves out, or passes away.

Understanding the variety of real estate loans accessible to you is a vital component in identifying the optimal financing strategy for your specific needs. Assessing your financial situation, credit history, and property objectives will help you select the appropriate loan type, setting you on a path towards a successful investment experience.

The Advantages and Disadvantages of Using REITs as a Source of Financing

Navigating the world of real estate project financing can be a hassle, and choosing to work with REITs offers a unique set of pros and cons. Grasping these aspects can assist you in making the best decision for your situation.

The Benefits

1. Capital availability: REITs can grant developers access to a more substantial pool of funds thanks to their ability to attract investment from numerous sources. This proves particularly useful for large-scale projects, which might be difficult for smaller developers to finance on their own.

2. Rapid funding: Being publicly-traded entities, REITs are often able to secure capital faster than traditional financing avenues like bank loans or private equity.

3. Reduced capital costs: REITs generally have more favorable borrowing costs compared to other financing options, which may make them a more cost-efficient choice for developers. Lower project expenses can translate into higher returns on investment.

The Drawbacks

1. Decreased control: A partnership with a REIT may require developers to give up some control over project management and decision-making. This can pose a challenge for developers who value having full autonomy over their projects.

2. Ownership dilution: REITs typically receive an equity share in the project in return for financing. This can lead to diluted ownership for the developer and potentially decrease their portion of the project's future earnings.

3. Rigorous requirements: To safeguard investor interests, REITs might impose strict conditions and guidelines on financed projects. These stipulations can restrict a developer's freedom in areas such as design, construction, and overall project execution.

Employing REITs to finance real estate projects comes with its own set of advantages and challenges. Developers and investors must carefully evaluate the specific benefits and drawbacks associated with partnering with a REIT. Aspects such as capital availability, rapid funding, and reduced capital costs should be balanced against potential downsides like decreased control, ownership dilution, and rigorous requirements.

Key Takeaways

- Utilizing leverage in real estate finance empowers investors to magnify potential returns with borrowed funds.

- Comprehending the time value for money is vital for appraising the current worth of future cash flows and evaluating investments.

- Achieving a balance between risk and reward is essential for cultivating a thriving real estate investment portfolio.

- Grasping cash flow fundamentals is crucial for smart real estate investment choices.

- A diverse array of funding sources exists for real estate projects, presenting flexible options and opportunities for growth.

Chapter Summary

The discussion in this chapter explored the core principles of real estate finance, emphasizing the significance of leverage and understanding the time value of money. Additionally, the necessity for a carefully managed risk-reward relationship and the importance of cash flow comprehension in making investment decisions were underscored. This chapter examined various financing options for real estate endeavors, such as real estate syndication, self-directed IRAs, and mezzanine financing, among others. It also described an assortment of real estate loan types, including conventional loans, bridge loans, and construction loans, to help investors pinpoint suitable financing approaches for their individual needs.

As we progress, it's vital to address the ethical aspects of engaging with REITs. The upcoming chapter will investigate environmental sustainability, social accountability, and equitable treatment of tenants and stakeholders.

CHAPTER 13

Ethics and Governance in REITs

In looking for people to hire, look for three qualities: integrity, intelligence, and energy. And if they don't have the first, the other two will kill you.

–Warren Buffett

Achieving financial goals is commendable, but it's also essential to evaluate the moral ramifications of real estate investments, which profoundly influence our world and communities.

In this chapter, we'll delve into the ethical dimensions of REITs. We'll study corporate governance in REITs, analyzing its function and the duties of boards of directors, management, and shareholders. Lastly, we'll explore the vital role that regulatory bodies like the SEC and FINRA play in nurturing a conscientious and prosperous investment environment.

Ethical Considerations for REITs

In the world of investing, it's essential to ponder the ethical implications of investment choices, REITs included. Striving for a balance between intelligent financial choices and contributing positively to society and the environment is key. To evaluate the ethical dimensions of REIT investments, center on these three core components: environmental sustainability, social responsibility, and equitable treatment of tenants and stakeholders (*REITs and social*, n.d.):

- Environmental sustainability: Real estate development and management have far-reaching and notable impacts on the environment. Evaluating the environmental policies and practices of potential REIT investments is crucial.

  A conscientious REIT will emphasize sustainable methods such as energy efficiency, water conservation, and waste reduction. They should also strive to reduce their environmental impact by employing eco-conscious construction and property management techniques. Assessing a REIT's dedication to green building certifications like LEED or BREEAM can offer valuable information about its commitment to environmental responsibility.

- Social responsibility: A critical factor when gauging the ethical standing of a REIT is its societal impact. Social responsibility encompasses diverse issues, including fair labor practices, community engagement, and support for affordable housing.

  Prior to investing, examine the REIT's labor policies and practices to ensure fair treatment and safe work environments for employees. Additionally, consider the REIT's community involvement, such as job creation or backing community development initiatives. A socially responsible REIT will prioritize the welfare of the communities in which it operates, nurturing positive connections with local residents and businesses.

- Equitable treatment of tenants and stakeholders: The well-being of tenants and other stakeholders is an important consideration for responsible investors. REITs should emphasize tenant welfare by providing safe, healthy, and reasonably priced living spaces. Delve into the REIT's tenant policies, concentrating on their dedication to maintenance, attentiveness to tenant issues, and just rent practices.

  Ethical REITs should also foster transparent relationships with stakeholders, including investors, suppliers, and government entities. Open communication and transparency cultivate trust and accountability, ensuring the REIT operates in the best interests of all stakeholders.

Remember that investments have the ability to mold the world. Choose prudently and invest in a future that resonates with your values. By concentrating on environmental sustainability, social responsibility, and equitable treatment of tenants and stakeholders, informed, ethical decisions can be made when investing in REITs. Keep these factors in mind while exploring real estate investing, and the journey towards building a portfolio that mirrors both financial objectives and personal values will be smoother.

Corporate Governance in REITs

Corporate governance is the unsung hero behind a company's operations and decision-making. Masterfully harmonizing the priorities of shareholders, management, customers, suppliers, financiers, the government, and the community, corporate governance is essential.

REITs, as distinct investment instruments, depend on solid corporate governance to thrive. These reasons all center on one core principle: trust. Investors placing their hard-earned money in REITs must have an assurance that their best interests are safeguarded. After all, no investor wants their assets to vanish due to poor management.

A critical element of corporate governance in REITs is an independent board of directors. These individuals oversee the company's management, ensuring shareholders' interests remain the top priority. By having a majority of independent directors, REITs can steer clear of conflicts of interest and preserve investor confidence. Additionally, this group helps shape the company's strategy, evaluates risks, and monitors performance; they're essentially the guardians.

> Transparency is another essential component of corporate governance in REITs. By sharing clear and accurate information about the company's financial situation, operations, and strategy with shareholders, trust between the company and its investors is fostered.

Furthermore, transparency holds the company accountable for

its actions, making it difficult to conceal any underhanded activities from shareholders.

Strong corporate governance also calls for rigorous risk management practices. In the realm of REITs, risk management is particularly crucial, as real estate investments face various challenges, such as market shifts, regulatory alterations, and natural disasters. An all-encompassing risk management system is needed to pinpoint, evaluate, and address these risks, ensuring the company's financial stability and safeguarding shareholders' investments.

Ethics—a topic worth revisiting—plays a considerable role in corporate governance. Companies with a robust ethical culture are more likely to earn and retain investor trust. Corporate governance sets the foundation for a company's ethical framework, holding management accountable for their actions. By fostering a culture of honesty and responsibility, REITs can ensure their decisions align with the best interests of shareholders and other stakeholders.

To sum up, corporate governance is a vital force in the world of REITs. It nurtures trust, champions transparency, tackles risks, and cultivates a strong ethical culture.

The Responsibilities of REIT Boards of Directors, Management, and Shareholders

In every flourishing REIT, the board of directors, management, and shareholders form a synergistic alliance, working together to build a prosperous organization that benefits all parties involved.

It's crucial to recognize that the board of directors acts as a protector of shareholders' interests. They establish specialized committees, such as audit, compensation, and nominating committees, to thoroughly examine particular areas of the organization. Consequently, their expertise and meticulous approach enhance the board's decision-making process by tackling relevant issues.

Shifting the focus to the management team, these individuals are responsible for transforming the strategic vision set by the board of directors into tangible results. They execute daily operations and handle various tasks that keep the REIT running smoothly and efficiently. They juggle the day-to-day operations while cultivating and preserving vital connections with tenants, suppliers, and local communities. Keeping an eye on market trends, the management team spots opportunities for growth and evaluates risks that could affect the company's investments.

But what about the shareholders? As investors, they have a personal stake in the REIT's performance. They're not just passive observers; they have the power to influence the company's direction through their voting rights. Shareholders are encouraged to attend annual meetings and engage in conversation with the board and management, addressing questions and concerns while offering valuable feedback. This open communication promotes a culture of accountability within the REIT.

Remember our discussion on corporate governance in REITs?

It emphasized the importance of cooperation between the board of directors, management, and shareholders. By each party fulfilling its unique duties, they contribute to a more transparent and responsible organization that puts the interests of all stakeholders first.

So, to sum things up, each of these stakeholders plays a pivotal role in the triumph of a REIT. The board of directors shapes the strategic course and forms specialized committees. The management team puts that plan into action, handling daily operations and nurturing relationships with various stakeholders. Shareholders, meanwhile, act as watchdogs, providing valuable input and holding the company accountable by exercising their voting rights and staying involved in discussions with company leaders.

Through this powerful collaboration, these stakeholders build a stable and successful REIT, generating attractive long-term returns for investors and benefiting all involved.

The Role of Regulatory Bodies

Multiple regulatory bodies collaborate to ensure REITs operate within legal frameworks, provide essential disclosures, and maintain fair practices in the market to the advantage of investors. It's time to explore some of these vital entities.

The SEC stands out as a crucial institution dedicated to defending investors, upholding just and proficient markets, and cultivating conditions favorable for capital development. In the context of REITs, the SEC enforces adherence to reporting and disclosure requirements, promoting transparency and upholding the financial market's integrity.

Another crucial participant in REIT governance is the Financial Industry Regulatory Authority (FINRA). Although not a government entity, FINRA acts as a self-regulatory organization, supervising brokerage firms and their registered representatives. FINRA's concern for REITs centers on the sale of non-traded REIT shares. By scrutinizing these transactions, FINRA ensures brokers and financial advisors comply with appropriate sales practices and offer accurate information about the risks and potential rewards of investing in non-traded REITs. Such oversight aids in shielding investors from possible fraud while preserving the integrity of the REIT market.

Beyond the SEC and FINRA, jurisdiction-specific regulatory bodies may come into play, depending on a REIT's location. For instance, in the United States, state-level securities regulators have the authority to govern particular aspects of REIT operations. These state regulators confirm that REITs adhere to local laws and regulations, thus protecting investors' interests within their jurisdiction.

The Internal Revenue Service (IRS) plays a notable role in shaping REIT governance. Owing to the distinct tax benefits granted to REITs, they must meet particular requirements set forth by the IRS. These mandates involve distributing the aforementioned annual dividend and allocating a minimum of 75% of their entire assets to real estate investments. Through monitoring adherence to these standards, the IRS helps maintain the tax advantages that render REITs an attractive investment option.

In certain countries, additional regulatory authorities contribute to REIT governance. The Financial Conduct Authority (FCA) in the UK supervises REITs. They ensure these entities comply with the necessary rules and meet the standards to retain their REIT status.

Grasping the importance of regulatory bodies in the world of REITs is essential for anyone mulling over real estate investment trust opportunities. Key organizations, such as the SEC, FINRA, state securities regulators, and the IRS, join forces to protect investors, uphold market integrity, and confirm REITs operate within the boundaries of the law.

Key Takeaways

- Prioritize REITs that champion environmental stewardship, as evidenced by green accreditations like LEED or BREEAM.

- Evaluate a REIT's commitment to social accountability by looking into its labor standards, local community support, and availability of affordable housing.

- For a reliable and responsible REIT, transparent dialogue and a cooperative attitude with stakeholders are key.

- Robust corporate governance in a REIT requires a

balanced board, straightforward messaging, meticulous risk oversight, and unwavering ethical convictions.

- A thriving and conscientious REIT depends on the collaborative efforts of the board of directors, management, and shareholders.

Chapter Summary

This chapter investigated the ethical dimensions that play a significant role in REIT investments, focusing on environmental awareness, social accountability, and fair treatment of all participants. Furthermore, this chapter accentuated the pivotal function of corporate governance in cultivating trust, promoting transparency, and navigating risks while adhering to ethical norms. The interplay between the board of directors, management, and shareholders was also analyzed, demonstrating how their collective endeavors contribute to a more transparent, responsible, and prosperous organization.

BONUS!

10 Ways to Win When Investing

10 Tips to Diversify Your REIT Portfolio

Creating a diversified REIT portfolio is essential for managing risk and optimizing returns. Here are ten tips for building a balanced and varied investment in real estate through REITs:

1. Distribute investments among various property categories: Allocate your funds to a mix of property classes, such as residential, commercial, industrial, and healthcare properties. This approach minimizes risk, as distinct sectors react differently to market shifts and economic phases.

2. Prioritize geographic variety: Spreading your investments across multiple geographic regions can help limit potential risks. Diverse regions experience economic expansion and contraction at different times, so exposure to a broad range of areas offers protection against local downturns.

3. Explore international REITs: In addition to domestic REITs, consider options in global markets. Expanding your investments internationally can provide access to

new growth opportunities and decrease the impact of country-specific economic occurrences on your portfolio.

4. Assess the management team's expertise: A competent, seasoned management team is crucial for a REIT's success. Investigate the qualifications and accomplishments of the leaders, as their decisions can significantly affect the REIT's performance and your potential returns.

5. Scrutinize the tenant mix: A varied tenant base lowers the risk of income loss due to vacancies or tenant insolvencies. Seek REITs with a range of tenants from diverse industries and evaluate their credit standing and lease terms.

6. Examine the REIT's financial stability: Analyze essential financial indicators, such as the debt-to-equity ratio, funds from operations, and dividend yield. A financially robust REIT with a low debt-to-equity ratio and a strong FFO signals an increased ability to endure economic challenges and generate income for shareholders.

7. Consider growth strategies: REITs can expand through acquisitions, development initiatives, or rent hikes. Evaluate the management's growth plan and its viability, given the current market conditions. A well-founded strategy that aligns with market tendencies can result in superior long-term returns.

8. Keep tabs on macroeconomic factors: Monitor broader economic aspects like interest rates, inflation, and the general state of the real estate market. These elements can impact the performance of REITs, so staying informed enables you to make more educated investment choices.

9. Embrace a range of investment approaches: Enhance the diversity of your REIT portfolio by integrating various investment tools, such as ETFs, mutual funds, and individual REIT equities. This tactic allows you to distribute risk and gain exposure to different sectors and management approaches.

10. Periodically adjust your portfolio: Frequently review your REIT portfolio to ensure it remains diverse and aligned with your investment objectives. Market conditions evolve, and adjusting your holdings can help you maintain an ideal blend of assets while managing risk.

Establishing a diversified REIT portfolio is a vital strategy for risk management and return optimization. By investing in an array of property types, locations, and investment vehicles, you can create a resilient and comprehensive real estate investment.

10 Tips to Research the REIT Market

Thoroughly researching the REIT market is vital for making well-founded investment choices. Use these ten tips to navigate the world of REITs and deepen your understanding of this unique investment sphere.

1. Grasp the nuances of REIT sectors: Get acquainted with different REIT sectors, including residential, retail, office, industrial, and healthcare properties. Each sector exhibits distinct market behaviors, growth potential, and risk factors, which can impact your investment decisions.

2. Stay informed on industry tendencies: Keep up with the real estate's industry trends, such as shifts in consumer habits, technological advancements, and regulatory changes. Comprehending these trends can help you pinpoint potential opportunities and risks in the REIT market.

3. Consider macroeconomic factors: Elements like interest rates, inflation, and GDP growth can influence the REIT market's performance. Regularly assess these indicators to identify potential challenges or supportive conditions for the sector.

4. Investigate financial performance measures: Examine crucial financial metrics for REITs, such as funds from operations, adjusted funds from operations (AFFO), dividend yield, and debt-to-equity ratio. These measures can offer insights into a REIT's financial stability and growth prospects.

5. Scrutinize the management team: A competent, experienced management team is essential for a REIT's

success. Delve into the backgrounds and accomplishments of the leaders, as their expertise and decision-making can substantially affect the REIT's performance.

6. Review the property portfolio: Inspect each REIT's property portfolio to gain insights into the quality, location, and diversification of its holdings. A well-managed and varied property portfolio can mitigate risk and enhance growth potential.

7. Evaluate tenant quality and leasing agreements: Examine the tenant mix and leasing terms of each REIT to gauge the reliability of rental income. A varied tenant base with long-term leases and robust credit profiles can generate more dependable revenue streams.

8. Compare REITs in the same sector: Benchmark REITs plays against their peers in the same sector to discern relative strengths and weaknesses. This comparative analysis can help you determine which REITs may be better suited to seize market opportunities or weather economic downturns.

9. Track REIT-focused analysts and publications: Follow industry experts, analysts, and publications specializing in the REIT market. These resources can provide invaluable insights, analyses, and updates that can inform your investment choices.

10. Immerse yourself in industry gatherings and activities: Take part in conferences, webinars, and various industry

happenings to remain up-to-date on recent trends, advancements, and prospects in the REIT market. Networking with industry professionals can offer unique perspectives and insights that might not be accessible through conventional research methods.

In-depth research on the REIT market is indispensable for making prudent investment decisions. By familiarizing yourself with REIT sectors, monitoring industry trends, and evaluating macroeconomic indicators, you can gain a better understanding of the market's potential risks and opportunities.

10 Tips to Pick the Best REITs

Employing the right strategy can help you pinpoint the top REIT contenders. Here are ten suggestions to assist you in making well-founded choices when selecting the finest REITs:

1. Grasp the REIT's sector specialization: Pay attention to the specific sector a REIT focuses on, such as residential, retail, office, or industrial properties. Each sector has distinct market behaviors, growth potential, and risk factors that can affect the REIT's overall performance.

2. Scrutinize financial performance: Investigate essential financial metrics like funds from operations (FFO), adjusted funds from operations (AFFO), dividend yield, and debt-to-equity ratio. These measures can reveal a

REIT's financial stability, growth prospects, and reliability.

3. Appraise the management team: A proficient and experienced management team is vital for a REIT's success. Delve into the backgrounds and achievements of the leaders, as their expertise and decision-making can significantly impact the REIT's performance.

4. Inspect the property portfolio: Examine a REIT's property portfolio to gain insights into the quality, location, and diversification of its holdings. An effectively managed and varied property portfolio can mitigate risk and enhance growth potential.

5. Review tenant quality and lease agreements: Assess the tenant mix and leasing terms of a REIT to gauge the reliability of rental income. A varied tenant base with long-term leases and robust credit profiles can generate more dependable revenue streams.

6. Contrast REITs within the same sector: Benchmark REITs against their peers in the same sector to discern relative strengths and weaknesses. This comparative analysis can help you determine which REITs may be better suited to seize market opportunities or weather economic downturns.

7. Reflect on dividend consistency and growth: A stable and increasing dividend is an appealing attribute for investors seeking income. Analyze the dividend history

and payout ratio of a REIT to evaluate its capacity to maintain and grow dividend payments over time.

8. Identify a competitive edge: Determine any competitive advantages a REIT may possess over its rivals, such as prime property locations, inventive business strategies, or solid tenant relationships. A competitive advantage can enable a REIT to outperform competitors and yield better returns for investors.

9. Observe macroeconomic factors: Monitor macroeconomic elements like interest rates, inflation, and GDP growth, which can influence the REIT market's performance. Comprehending these factors can help you make informed investment decisions and anticipate potential challenges or supportive conditions for the sector.

10. Commit to ongoing research and due diligence: The process of choosing the best REITs necessitates continuous research and due diligence. Stay current on industry trends, company news, and financial performance to ensure well-informed decisions and the ability to adjust your investment strategy as needed.

Selecting the ideal REITs for your investment portfolio entails understanding the sector focus, delving into financial performance, and evaluating the management team and property portfolio. By following these ten suggestions, you can be better prepared to spot the most promising REITs and optimize your investment portfolio.

10 Tips to Improve Yields vs. Capital Appreciation

Striking the ideal balance between yield and capital appreciation is essential for optimizing your portfolio's performance. Here are ten tips to mull over when comparing yield-focused investments to those that emphasize capital appreciation:

1. Clarify your investment aims: Start by identifying your investment priorities. Are you seeking steady income or long-term growth? Knowing your goals will help you determine the appropriate balance between yield and capital appreciation in your investment strategy.

2. Evaluate your risk appetite: Yield-focused investments, like dividend stocks or bonds, usually have less volatility compared to growth-oriented investments. By understanding your risk tolerance, you can decide on the perfect mix of income-generating and capital appreciation investments.

3. Think about your investment timeframe: Consider the time you have for your investments. If your investment horizon is longer, you might be able to take on more risk and concentrate on capital appreciation. On the other hand, if you're nearing retirement, prioritizing yield could be more suitable.

4. Keep tax implications in mind: Various investments may have differing tax consequences. For instance, dividend income and capital gains might be subject to distinct tax

rates. Take these implications into account when balancing yield and capital appreciation in your portfolio.

5. Diversify among asset classes: A well-rounded portfolio can help you achieve the right blend of yield and capital appreciation. Incorporate a range of asset classes, such as stocks, bonds, and real estate, to capitalize on their unique return and risk characteristics.

6. Examine past performance: Study the historical performance of yield- and capital appreciation-focused investments to gain insights into potential future returns. While past performance doesn't guarantee future results, it can offer valuable context when weighing your choices.

7. Keep an eye on economic factors: Economic elements, like interest rates, inflation, and GDP growth, can affect the relative appeal of yield and capital appreciation investments. Monitor these factors to make informed decisions regarding your portfolio's composition.

8. Understand sector dynamics: Different sectors may provide varying opportunities for yield and capital appreciation. For example, specific sectors might be more conducive to dividend payouts, while others may have higher growth potential. Grasping these dynamics can help you select investments that align with your objectives.

9. Consult with professionals: Seeking advice from a

financial advisor or investment expert can offer valuable insights and guidance when balancing yield and capital appreciation. They can help you navigate intricate investment decisions and customize a strategy tailored to your particular needs.

10. Periodically review your portfolio: Consistently assess your investment portfolio to ensure it remains in line with your goals, risk tolerance, and investment horizon. This may involve rebalancing your holdings occasionally to maintain the desired mix of yield and capital appreciation investments.

Contemplating yields versus capital appreciation requires you to evaluate your investment goals, risk tolerance, and investment horizon. Moreover, factoring in tax implications, diversifying across asset classes, and analyzing historical performance can help you find the right balance.

10 Tips to Manage Fees

To optimize your returns and make your hard-earned money work effectively for you, it's essential to manage fees linked to your REIT investments. Here are ten tips to help you stay on top of REIT fees:

1. Grasp fee structures: Get acquainted with different fees tied to REIT investments, such as management fees, advisory fees, and transaction costs. Understanding fee structures empowers you to make well-informed

decisions and evaluate various investment options.

2. Examine REITs closely: Investigate the fees of multiple REITs, taking into account not just the amounts but also their calculation methods. Comparing fees helps you pinpoint REITs that strike a favorable balance between cost and potential returns.

3. Assess passive and active management: Typically, passively managed REITs, like index funds or ETFs, have lower fees compared to actively managed funds. Identify whether passive or active management aligns better with your investment objectives, remembering that decreased fees can result in higher net returns.

4. Keep an eye on expense ratios: When investing in REIT funds, pay attention to the expense ratio, which represents the total yearly fund operating expenses as a percentage of the fund's assets. Generally, lower expense ratios mean fewer deductions from your investment returns.

5. Try negotiating: If you're investing through a financial advisor or investment manager, explore the possibility of fee negotiations. Although not always feasible, negotiating can lead to cost savings and ultimately boost your investment returns.

6. Seek fee discounts: Watch for promotions like reduced fees for new investors or for investing a specific amount. Discounts can assist you in saving money and enhancing your REIT investments' overall performance.

7. Weigh performance against fees: Evaluate your REIT investments' performance relative to the fees you're paying. If an investment is underperforming but charging substantial fees, it might be worth investigating other options that offer better value.

8. Employ dollar-cost averaging: Dollar-cost averaging involves consistently investing a fixed sum of money, irrespective of market conditions. This approach can help you manage transaction costs by spreading them out over time instead of making large, infrequent investments.

9. Choose a fee-based advisor: If working with a financial advisor, opt for a fee-based advisor over one who charges commissions. Fee-based advisors receive a set amount for their services, helping ensure their recommendations aren't influenced by potential commissions from selling specific investments.

10. Review your portfolio routinely: Periodically assess your REIT investments to confirm you're getting the best value for your money. This may involve reallocating your investments or adjusting your investment strategy to minimize fees and maximize returns.

To sum up, managing REIT fees requires understanding fee structures, closely examining different REITs, and considering passive versus active management. Furthermore, staying mindful of expense ratios, attempting to negotiate when possible, and looking for fee discounts can lead to savings.

Conclusion

The individual investor should act consistently as an investor and not as a speculator.

–Ben Graham

As the adventure through real estate investment trusts comes to an end, take a moment to reflect on the information and wisdom gained throughout this journey. Delving into the world of REITs, this book has illuminated their historical background, diverse types, advantages, investment methods, performance assessment, portfolio creation strategies, and much more.

The beauty of REITs lies in the unique opportunity they provide for investors like you to engage with the real estate market without being burdened by direct property ownership. With a wide array of REIT types to choose from, you can explore different sectors and geographical locations, enabling a degree of diversification that's challenging to achieve with conventional real estate investments. Factor in the liquidity and accessibility of REITs, and you've got yourself a versatile investment instrument that's both manageable and flexible.

Moving forward, it's essential to understand that the future of REITs is intrinsically linked to the expansion and metamorphosis of the worldwide real estate industry. As new possibilities and hurdles surface, you must remain vigilant and well-informed to seize these emerging opportunities. Progress in technology, evolving economic landscapes, and the development of market dynamics will indubitably mold the future of the REIT industry, and those who can adapt to these changes are more likely to succeed.

This book aspires to equip you with valuable insights and a robust foundation to enable you to confidently traverse the world of REITs. By grasping the potential risks and rewards, employing astute investment tactics, and staying current with the latest trends and advancements, you can unlock the power of REITs to attain your financial objectives.

REITs can feel daunting initially but remember that every successful investor takes that first step. Start by understanding your financial aspirations and evaluating your risk tolerance. This foundation will empower you to make well-informed choices, select suitable REITs, and establish a diversified portfolio that aligns with your distinct goals.

On this thrilling investment adventure, don't hesitate to seek guidance and support. Connecting with fellow investors and learning from their experiences can offer priceless insights as you traverse this dynamic market. Avoid letting the fear of missing out or the temptation of short-term gains influence your decisions.

As your confidence in investing grows, explore new prospects, and broaden your horizons. The world of real estate investment trusts is extensive and varied, and as the market progresses, there will undoubtedly be novel and inventive ways to capitalize on your REIT investments. Maintain your curiosity and always be on the lookout for exceptional opportunities that resonate with your financial goals and principles.

In conclusion, the time has come for you to grab control and venture into the captivating sphere of real estate investment trusts. Armed with the precious knowledge and insights from this book, you're well-prepared to start making informed decisions and crafting a REIT portfolio tailored to your needs. The journey might present challenges, but with perseverance, discipline, and a dash of courage, you can undoubtedly achieve remarkable things in REIT investing.

So, Carpe Diem (it means "seize the day!" if you haven't seen Dead Poets Society). Utilize the wisdom you've acquired and begin forging your path in the dynamic world of REITs. As you embark on this expedition, stay committed to your goals, remain adaptable, and seize the opportunities for growth and learning that await. Here's to your success and prosperity in the exhilarating realm of real estate investment trusts!

Glossary

Benchmark: The go-to gauge for sizing up your investments against the market's performance. It's like a financial check-up, helping you see whether your money moves are winning or could use a little extra oomph.

Diversification: A savvy method for managing investment risks by spreading your money across a mix of assets or sectors, softening the blow of any underperformers, and aiming for steadier returns.

Dividend: Payments in cash or additional shares from a company or investment vehicle (e.g., REIT) to its shareholders, originating from earnings. Regular dividends contribute to financial stability.

Income: The earnings generated from an investment, business, or asset. In real estate, income sources include rent payments, loan interest, or selling a property at a higher price than its purchase cost. Steady income, such as dividends or rent, can provide financial security.

Interest: The price tag of borrowing money or the enticing perk you receive for saving or investing your dough. Interest rates can be fickle, but harnessing the might of compound interest could transform your savings into a flourishing financial garden.

Investment Strategy: A tailored plan for choosing and supervising investments, considering your financial goals, risk acceptance, and the timeframe you have at your disposal.

Legal: The set of principles, statutes, and norms that bring order and fairness to our money matters. Covering everything from agreements to property ownership, tax legislation to finance rules, and staying in the loop on legal issues is key to thriving financially.

Leverage: Harnessing borrowed capital for real estate investments with the expectation that property appreciation will outstrip borrowing expenses, paving the way for potentially boosted returns.

Metrics: Tools used to assess and distinguish REITs based on their performance, financial stability, and market worth.

Potential: The promising prospects and opportunities associated with an investment, business, or asset. In real estate, the potential may refer to growth, development, or value appreciation influenced by factors like market trends, location, and demand.

Regulation: The set of rules and guidelines governing how businesses, organizations, and individuals operate within a specific industry or area. Regulations aim to protect investors, consumers, and the environment, maintain financial system stability, and encourage fair competition. Compliance is crucial in real estate and investments to ensure transparency and safeguard all parties involved.

Revenue: The impressive haul of cash a business or individual collects by providing goods or services. Found at the top of an income statement, it shows the dough rolling in before costs, deductions, or taxes come into play.

Risks: The uncertainties or possible drawbacks associated with investing or starting a business. Risks can arise from market changes, economic conditions, or new regulations. Considering and managing risks is essential when making investment decisions.

Tax: The way governments gather funds from what you earn to keep public services, such as schools, roads, and parks, up and running. Nobody's thrilled about it, but it's essential for a well-functioning community.

Trade-Off: The process of balancing the advantages and disadvantages of various metrics while examining and comparing REITs for potential investment opportunities.

References

A guide to real estate development. (n.d.). Prologis. https://www.prologis.com/what-we-do/resources/guide-real-estate-development

Benjamin Franklin quotes. (n.d.). Brainy Quote. https://www.brainyquote.com/quotes/benjamin_franklin_129817

CFI Team. (2023, January 8). *P/FFO.* CFI. https://corporatefinanceinstitute.com/resources/commercial-real-estate/p-ffo/#:~:text=P%2FFFO%2C%20or%20Price%20to,on%20the%20sale%20of%20properties.

CFI Team. (2023, January 19). *Private REITs vs publicly traded REITs.* CFI. https://corporatefinanceinstitute.com/resources/commercial-real-estate/private-reits-vs-publicly-traded-reits/

Chen, J. (2023, April 5). *Real estate investment trust (REIT): How they work and how to invest.* Investopedia. https://www.investopedia.com/terms/r/reit.asp

Copeland, G. (2021, November 27). *How liquid are REITs?.* Realized.

https://www.google.com/amp/s/www.realized1031.com/blog/how-liquid-are-reits%3fhs_amp=true

DeBree, P. J. (n.d.). *UPREITs and downREITs gain popularity*. CCIM. https://www.ccim.com/cire-magazine/articles/upreits-and-downreits-gain-popularity/

Eleanor Roosevelt quotes. (n.d.). Brainy Quote. https://www.brainyquote.com/quotes/eleanor_roosevelt_100940

Eve. (n.d.). *Famous quotes about real estate*. Agent Image. https://www.google.com/amp/s/www.agentimage.com/blog/famous-quotes-about-real-estate/amp/

Harper, R. D. (2022, June 2). *How to analyze REITs (real estate investment trusts)*. Investopedia. https://www.investopedia.com/articles/04/030304.asp

History of REITs & real estate investing. (n.d.). Nareit. https://www.reit.com/what-reit/history-reits

In looking for people to hire, look for three qualities: integrity, intelligence and energy. And if they don't have the first, the other two will kill you. (n.d.). AZ Quotes. https://www.azquotes.com/quote/522299

Jason Hollands. (2000, March 27). *"Know what you own and know why you own it"*. The Guardian. https://www.google.com/amp/s/amp.theguardian.co

m/money/2000/mar/27/1#bsht=CgVic2hocBIECA
MwAg

Joseph, E. (2022, May 25). *5 expert insight on real estate investing.*
Purple Living. https://purpleliving.xyz/blog/5-expert-
insight-on-real-estate-investing.

Litvak, E. (2021, July 29). *Real estate development 101: the myths, the
realities and how to get started.* Forbes.
https://www.google.com/amp/s/www.forbes.com/sit
es/forbesrealestatecouncil/2021/07/29/real-estate-
development-101-the-myths-the-realities-and-how-to-
get-started/amp/

Mark Twain quotes. (n.d.). Brainy Quote.
https://www.brainyquote.com/quotes/mark_twain_3
80355

Marquit, M. (2023, January 5). *How to invest in real estate with
REITs.* Forbes.
https://www.forbes.com/advisor/investing/how-to-
invest-in-reits/

REITs and Social Impact. (n.d.). Nareit.
https://www.reit.com/investing/reits-
sustainability/reits-and-social-impact

REITs prove resilient in great recession. (n.d.). Nareit.
https://www.reit.com/node/120379

REITs widen their global reach. (n.d.). Nareits.
https://www.reit.com/news/reit-magazine/march-
april-2022/reits-widen-their-global-reach

Real estate cannot be lost or stolen, nor can it be carried away. Purchased with common sense, paid for in full, and managed with reasonable care, it is about the safest investment in the world. (n.d.). AZ Quotes. https://www.azquotes.com/quote/628914

Real estate investment trust. (n.d.). Wikipedia. https://en.m.wikipedia.org/wiki/Real_estate_investment_trust

Richard Branson quotes. (n.d.). Brainy Quote. https://www.brainyquote.com/quotes/richard_branson_452112

Robert Kiyosaki quotes. (n.d.). Brainy Quote. https://www.brainyquote.com/quotes/robert_kiyosaki_626868

Ruth, A. (2021, February 18). *Ben Graham – be an investor not a speculator.* Due. https://due.com/ben-graham-be-an-investor-not-a-speculator/

Ruth, A. (2022, June 13). *Paul Samuelson – investing is like watching grass grow.* Due. https://due.com/paul-samuelson-investing-is-like-watching-grass-grow/

20 famous real estate investing quotes. (n.d.). Realty Mogul. https://www.realtymogul.com/knowledge-center/article/20-famous-real-estate-investing-quotes

Weber, M. (2019, June 26). *Ben Graham: "In the short run, the market is a voting machine but in the long run it is a weighing machine."* LinkedIn. https://www.linkedin.com/pulse/ben-graham-short-run-market-voting-machine-long-weighing-weber?trk=read_related_article-card_title